Why Are You
Shouting At Us?

The dos and don'ts of
behaviour management

ALSO AVAILABLE FROM BLOOMSBURY EDUCATION

Getting the Buggers to Behave (4th edition), Sue Cowley
The Behaviour Guru, Tom Bennett
100 Ideas for Managing Behaviour, Johnnie Young

Why Are You Shouting At Us?

The dos and don'ts of behaviour management

Phil Beadle and John Murphy

B L O O M S B U R Y

LONDON • NEW DELHI • NEW YORK • SYDNEY

Published 2013 by Bloomsbury Education
Bloomsbury Publishing plc
50 Bedford Square, London WC1B 3DP
www.bloomsbury.com

9781441185150

3 5 7 9 10 8 6 4 2

Typeset by Fakenham Prepress Solutions, Fakenham, Norfolk NR21 8NN
Printed and bound by CPI Group (UK) Ltd, Croydon CR0 4YY

This book is produced using paper that is made from wood grown in
managed, sustainable forests. It is natural, renewable and recyclable.
The logging and manufacturing processes conform to the environmental
regulations of the country of origin.

To Ken Beadle: My dad.

To my wife Kate and children Tom and Gisele

for making my life complete.

Contents

Acknowledgements

Phil Beadle: Rob Cooper: my mate, without whom this book would not have existed.

John Murphy: Dr Jonty Clarke for all you have taught me and to all the staff teams I have worked with that have made such a difference for so many children.

Foreword

The aim of the authors in writing this book is 'to give you the tools to influence the behaviour in your classroom so that it is outstanding.' Their aim is straight and true. Bullseye!

There are many books on managing challenging behaviour that offer 'techniques' for getting children to respond appropriately. This isn't one of them. The problem with techniques is that few people respond to getting 'techniqued'. Have you ever felt a connection, a sense of rapport, with the underpaid cold caller on the end of the phone who is instructed to read off their cue card no matter what you are saying? So it is with techniques.

By contrast, this book offers teachers an understanding of what it is like to be a child in school today and what it takes to help them thrive. It underpins this understanding with compassion and humanity. It draws on accessible psychology to reinforce what is evidentially incontestable – the behaviour, values and habits of the adult are the most significant factors in classroom success. There are very few books on this subject that grab you warmly by the throat, keeping its thumbs out of the way (it'll make sense when you've read it) and lead you on a reflective journey that is as uncomfortably challenging as it is enlightening and uplifting. Of those, this is one of the best yet. There is something quite special about the insights, attitudes and skills shared on these pages. I was impressed from start to finish by the common sense, pragmatic and proven approaches and the way they are firmly rooted in the context of modern classroom life. I wince a little when I recall thinking to myself whilst reading the draft, 'This is fantastic – you'd never get this kind of stuff in a book.'

John and Phil have captured so much of their accumulated wisdom and experience here and with such clarity that reading it feels like a personal mentoring session from them. In psychological terms they are both supremely consciously competent.

It pulls no punches; it is the (extremely well-researched) world according to John and Phil; but when you tune into the passion and emotional intelligence with which they approach the topic, it is a world all teachers should seriously be looking to at least visit or better still emigrate to. How many books on challenging behaviour endorse love, understanding and trust and explicitly stated expectations as having an impact within the first four pages?

What helps this book to be so useful and informative is the way in which the reader is both challenged about their thinking – the initial audit and the way in which we return to it after each chapter – and scaffolded in their learning. In the many scenarios covered that teachers regularly face, John and Phil suggest what to do, describe how to do it and crucially explain why it's a good idea. The 'what', 'how' and 'why' are the essential components of establishing a habit. In a survey of NQTs I conducted over the past 12 months, 68% felt ill-equipped by their training for life in the classroom. This book has the potential to make significant inroads into this issue.

It is always best to leave it to the authors to capture the essence of their own book. They state that, *'Real behaviour management is about guiding a student to understand, own and anticipate the consequences of their own behaviour and to learn a range of strategies to adapt that will help them manage their lives successfully despite the challenges they face.'*

It doesn't get much more real than this book.

Andy Vass, 2012

Introduction

There have been times while we have been working alongside each other on this book that we've experienced moments that it would not be reaching too far in the direction of hyperbole to describe as having been rapturous.

There have been moments when we have been – as comfortable in each other's company as two people who have been friends for a number of years, and who have respect for each other, tend to be – utterly engaged in sharing and reflecting upon past experience; and we have learnt from each other, discovered new things about ourselves and felt sufficiently secure in our own shells to have formed nascent new ideas and, from thence, tried to influence the other's thinking.

One Saturday morning, during the early stages of planning the book, John coined a metaphor. Focusing his attention on a child's ball on a table in the crepuscular back room of Phil's place of residence, he said, 'If we are focusing on the ball, it is not you who is important; it is not me who is important; it is the ball.'

If we may overextend this metaphor a little so that we take the ball to be the learning and the achievement of the children you teach, then it isn't about you, and it isn't about them. It is about their learning. Learning is a collaborative task that involves you, the teacher, and them, the students, but it is not about either you or them. It is about the learning. You, like the authors of this book have been during the process of writing it, are working alongside the young people and you are all focusing on the same thing.

This transaction can be rapturous. And that is what we are after: moments where teacher and class work together in balletic symbiosis; where everyone is relaxed; in full control of themselves; and are in an aroused, heightened state, where they are so utterly engaged in what they are doing they lose all sense of time. This state, which Mihali Csikszentmihalyi defined as being *flow*, is when we are most happy and is life's ideal. (In an ideal world, or in an ideal educational environment, we would be in this state more or less all the time. Every lesson would leave students with a profound sense of loss as it ended.) It is at these moments of complete symbiosis that we reach for what Scottish intellectual Pat Kane describes as, 'The idea that group performance can somehow, at its best, reconcile unity and diversity.'[1]

The classroom, in the language of game theory, is a non-zero-sum game. Robert Wright, who invented the particular branch of mathematics that studies the interactions of systems, proposes two forms of games: zero-sum games, which are those at which there is an end point 'you win, you lose', and non-zero-sum games, in which there is no such defined end point. Educating children is a non-zero-sum game. As Pat Kane writes, 'It's open ended, accumulative and fruitfully messy, and it increases rewards for all those who commit to the exchange (despite occasional glitches and bad behaviour) over a long period.'[2]

However, and sadly, humans are rarely, if ever, an ideal version of themselves and there is no such thing as an ideal educational environment. You will work with students whose lives set them challenges that they are barely able to face, and these challenges will affect the way they behave in your lessons.

There are various schools of thought on behaviour. Some would argue, somewhat pessimistically, that behaviour is innate (genetic even). If this limiting judgement is correct, then you reading this book will be an exercise in pointlessness, and you should put it down straightaway and go and do something useful, since whatever you, as a teacher, do to influence the behaviour of your classes will have no effect. It cannot be changed and you should give up promptly.

The antithesis of this is the profoundly more optimistic 'behaviouralist' approach, which suggests that love, understanding and trust, combined with constantly and explicitly stated expectations, will impact on behaviour and that any student can possibly achieve any outcome. In essence we believe that behaviour can be learnt and can improve.

You might wonder whether the behaviouralist approach is potentially grasping a little too blindly at vapour. It is one thing being optimistic regarding the outcomes you might achieve for your students, but let's get

---

[1] Kane, 2005, p. 14.
[2] Kane, 2005, p. 59.

real: there are kids whose life experiences make them unreachable by the education system as it is, and by you as a teacher in particular.

A behaviouralist approach acknowledges that there are certain things that you are not going to be able to change about your students' existences. You cannot change their family, their family's value system and you cannot change their current economic situation (though we may change their economic future(s)). But you can underpin their experience at school in a way that mitigates and limits the impact of their home lives; you can treat your students in an emotionally intelligent way; you can display trust and you can show love; you can be a positive influence for good.

As an example of what the behaviouralist approach can achieve, here are two case studies based on experiences we have had with students we have worked alongside.

Andrew was from a single-parent family. When inducted into the school he appeared lucid, and responded entirely normally to cues. When confronted directly, however, he would switch almost instantaneously into highly aroused displays of extreme anger. He would smash objects, doors, whole rooms; he would physically attack teachers. At one point, when he was having to be physically restrained so that he didn't cause himself or anyone else serious damage, John whispered in his ear, 'What's up? Tell me.' And he broke down.

It transpired that his chief memory of early childhood was of witnessing his father attempting to murder his mother and, though the father hadn't succeeded, he had still managed to break her back. Andrew's every waking moment was devoted to attaining his ultimate ambition, which was to murder his father. He was given a job in the school mentoring other children who had anger management issues themselves.

Andrew is now employed as a full-time, paid mentor to those children.

Bruno suffered from sleep deficit syndrome and was born dependent on cocaine; he had complex learning needs and would spend three days at a time awake and by the third day he would be falling asleep on desks. He would then crash and burn and have to spend the next two-and-a-half days in bed. The solution to this was negotiated with the staff at school: it was to have him in school on the first two days of his waking cycle, and to ensure that he was properly fed on those days; the other days he would spend at home. When in school he would be asked to work in short bursts and the curriculum he was studying was differentiated, so that everything would be taught through the medium of his particular obsession: a love of animals.

Bruno eventually went to college to study animal husbandry.

What OFSTED says

OFSTED makes the distinction between behaviour being 'good' and behaviour being 'outstanding' in the following manner: where behaviour is 'good', it is because a teacher is managing it well; where behaviour is 'outstanding', it is because the students are managing it themselves.

Ask yourself, what happens when you walk out of the room? Does it all erupt into chaos, or do students continue working purposefully? Have you imposed a seating plan on the class, or have you given the students the criteria for the seating plan and asked them to work it out on their own? Where behaviour is 'outstanding', it is the students who set the cultural norms themselves. While the rules will be set by the teachers, it is the students who ensure they are followed.

As an example of how this can work: a dearly loved and respected former colleague of ours was having an issue with his son's behaviour and, as a result, had to move him to a new school. At his new school he began to limber up his naughty boy chops and gave out early signals that he was capable of some quite heavyweight naughtiness. He was taken aside by a classmate, who gently informed him, 'We don't do that kind of stuff here.' Our colleague's son immediately desisted. This example indicates how 'outstanding' behaviour operates: the students buy into the culture and the value system so completely that they actually police the upholding of the values.

Testing what you already know and evaluating what you have learnt

This book sets out the dos and don'ts of behaviour management and is designed to give you the tools to confidently influence the behaviour in your lessons so that it is 'outstanding'. That is what we are aiming for.

But in order to get somewhere you must first know where you are, judge the distance between where you are now and where you want to be, and then take steps to reduce that distance. The first step of the journey is seeing what you already know.

Complete the following questionnaire. (You will be tested on it at the end.) The object of the exercise is to identify your baseline knowledge and confidence in terms of managing behaviour. Read through the statements listed on the left-hand side and mark how confidently you can make each statement about yourself, if at all. If you don't understand the statement, mark 'Huh?'

The results will provide an audit of what you know now. Each section of the questionnaire represents a chapter of the book. After reading each chapter you will be asked to repeat the relevant section of the questionnaire, so be honest; then you can evaluate what you have learnt from just reading the book.

The aim, after having read the book and started to put into practice the behaviour management techniques we recommend, is for you to be able to very confidently assert each statement.

Test yourself

	Very confident	Confident	Not confident	Huh?
Are you who you should be internally?				
I am aware of my own value system.				
I know all the school rules on behaviour.				
I implement all the school rules on behaviour.				
I am consistent, and treat each situation on its particular merits.				
I display empathy easily.				
I am fair.				

Can you manage your own behaviour?				
I can analyse cycles of transmission and receipt.				
I am aware that my attitude affects my behaviour.				
I differentiate my behaviour for different students.				
I can break a faulty circle of transmission and receipt.				
I can conduct a behaviour impact analysis.				
I am aware of the full varieties of relationship that I will have to manage.				
I know why I shouldn't shout.				
I know why I shouldn't discuss confidential business in front of students.				
I know the differences between bonding and bridging relationships.				

Are you who you should be externally?				
I am aware of Mehrabian's ideas of 'liking'.				
I can convey 'liking' with my facial expressions.				
I know the difference between D smiles and non-D smiles.				
I know how to manage my facial expression when in conflict.				
I know where and how to stand when in front of a class.				
I know how to use my body when supporting a student.				
I know the difference between 'open' and 'closed' body language.				
I know the body language don'ts to avoid when in conflict.				
I know the body language dos when in conflict.				
I use positive touch.				

I am aware that, when physically intervening, thumbs do the damage.				
I am aware of cultural differences in gesture.				
I can use dynamic range.				
I drop my tone of voice in conflict situations.				
I know what language to avoid.				
I know what language to use.				
I present myself professionally.				
Do you understand your students' behaviour?				
I understand the pivotal importance of optimism in all situations.				
I know what causes reactive anger.				
I can recognize a trigger and remove it.				
I know the stages of arousal in anger.				
I can redirect student behaviour.				

I know how to conduct a risk assessment when anger erupts into violence.				
I know the law when anger erupts into violence.				
I can manage a recovery period.				
I can manage my own anger.				
Do you understand manipulative anger?				
I am aware of the difference between reactive and manipulative anger.				
I have strategies to deal with threats.				
I have strategies to deal with destructiveness.				
I have strategies to deal with bullying.				
I have strategies to deal with unjust blaming.				
I have strategies to deal with grandiosity.				
I have strategies to deal with vengefulness.				
I have strategies to deal with unpredictability.				

I know how passive anger manifests.				
I have strategies to deal with secretive behaviour.				
I have strategies to deal with psychological manipulation.				
I have strategies to deal with self-blame.				
I have strategies to deal with dispassionate behaviour.				
Can you use de-escalation techniques?				
I am aware that humour is the best de-escalation technique.				
I know how to stand between combatants.				
I have partnered up with another teacher to discuss behaviour management problems.				
I can model the behaviour I want to see.				
I am prepared to change the activity or location when an incident is in the build-up stage.				

I know how to praise recent positives.				
I am prepared to be silent during an incident.				
I set attainable boundaries.				
I extend or reduce personal space as appropriate.				
I am aware that it is sometimes appropriate to just 'let them get on with it'.				
I can use the 'ignore the behaviour and praise the person next to them' technique.				
I can judge when it is appropriate to guide a student away physically.				
I am aware of the dynamics of bringing other staff members into an incident.				
I am aware that 'mirroring behaviour' in a humorous manner can sometimes be effective.				
I listen.				

Can you use humour to create relationships?				
I can be self-deprecating.				
My classroom is a playful arena.				
I use humour to foster relationships.				
I am prepared to use humour when issuing sanctions.				
I am aware of the difference between 'good' and 'bad' humour.				

Chapter 1
Are you who you should be internally?

Values – who you are internally

The journey towards transforming behaviour in your class starts with you. First, let's take a look at how and why you came to be here. What are the *positive* reasons you chose teaching as a profession?

A helpful exercise is to write down the reasons and rank them in order of importance. As an example to guide you, here's one we did earlier.

In order of priority	Reasons
2	Political reasons
4	Enjoyment of being around young people
5	An interest in having intellectual stimulation
3	Passion for the life chances of young people
6	A commitment to education as a driver of social mobility
7	A desire to change things
1	Creativity
8	Service to the community
9	The money's not awful

Do your version of this exercise on the next page. Write down the reasons you first entered teaching, and then number them in the order of their importance.

In order of priority	Reasons

Having done so, you have now identified your core values; the rank you have given these on the continuum will tell you how far you are driven by these; the particular weight you ascribe to them.

You may well believe that you are not especially driven by a core set of values and that you are just doing a job in order to earn enough money to pay the landlord every month. You may even deny the concept of values, thinking it a geriatric term appropriate only for those who live in gated communities in the leafier parts of Surrey. But, whatever attitude you have towards the existence of a value system, you will still be in possession of one. (It may be rusty or covered in a thick film of dust, but it will certainly exist.) You will, for instance, have your own version of what is acceptable in terms of behaviour in the classroom. You will also have a sense of what you would want a teacher's behaviour to be like if your child were in their class (or, if you don't have children, if you were in that class as a child). Ask yourself a simple question: what are the values you'd hold if you were to really make a genuinely significant difference to the educational chances of the young people for whom you are responsible?

We, as the authors of this book and as educators, have our own sets of values. Phil answers the question thus:

> I am in a state of perpetual, raging anger at the injustices of the caste system in this country and the means through which those at the top arrange its perpetuation. For me, the fact that a child born in straitened circumstances will most likely die in those same circumstances is the most Grand Guignol of injustices and it is an injustice enshrined in

policy. Where I am able to counter this injustice through my interactions with young people – specifically, through making them believe they are capable of far more than they might otherwise have thought and through teaching them how to communicate with skill and with force – I take delight in being able to do so.

Education changes everything: your horizons, your enjoyment, your economic situation. I will continue to campaign until my death for the rights of the disenfranchised to receive an education that will allow them to compete with those who would seek to keep working-class children deliberately less well educated for their own ends.

John's values came about as an accident of his height:

I am six-foot-four, utterly bald and a black belt in various martial arts. My career started as the token male teacher in a primary school. I found behaviour easy to manage straightaway. I had an undeniable presence and students were all too willing to give me their attention. I was in control and it was easy.

As time moved on, however, and I became a father, my perception of managing behaviour changed completely. The discovery of the precious nature of paternal love – that my own children were the most precious things in the world to me – led me to the conviction that I should always treat my pupils with the same dignity, respect and parameters that I would want my own children to receive from their teachers.

In 2001, I was asked by a local authority to take over a special school for boys with emotional, behavioural and social problems. My previous confidence in my ability to control students' behaviour was revealed as a sham: the special school led me to the unfortunate discovery of the depths of my inadequacies. My life as a residential head with those young men for five years was humbling, and in that time I discovered that real compassion had to be combined with a version of the clichéd 'tough love' and an endless optimism, along with a commitment to the long haul. These were the real ingredients for success. For those young men to trust me, see me every day, be rewarded for doing the right thing, be able to laugh at my undeniable baldness and begin to laugh at themselves would allow them a chance to gain respect for themselves.

Real behaviour management is about guiding a student to understand, own and anticipate the consequences of their own behaviour and to learn a range of strategies to adapt that will help them manage their lives successfully despite the challenges they face.

The values you would want your own children's teachers to hold

It is not unreasonable to suggest that a human being of any merit would attempt to live – personally and professionally – in accordance with their value system (until something happens that causes us to modify that system – in which case we attempt to accommodate the subtle changes required to live in accordance with a subtly changed set of values). But look at it from another angle. Look at the classroom through the eyes of the parents. The vast majority of parents, as John has outlined above, view their children as 'the most precious things in the world', and they are entrusting you with their jewels in the hope that you will take care of them and hand them back shining. It is a phenomenal act of trust for a parent to leave their child with another adult, and it is a trust that is only likely to be rewarded in any fulfilled sense if the teacher holds tight the values that the parents would want their child's teachers to hold.

What are those values? An exhaustive list might take a year or two, but they certainly would not exclude the following: consistency, empathy and fairness.

Consistency

We all assume that we are experts in schools, since we've all been to school. We've all had (some) experience of life. We all have our own perceptions, aspirations and versions of what is acceptable. The point is that what is acceptable in an organic organization like a school must be an agglomeration of what everyone within that institution finds acceptable. It must be a shared value system to which everyone, including the students, subscribes. You may value your personal eccentricities, thinking, perhaps, that they add colour to a world too easily faded into monochrome. You may feel that consistency is a concept too far lodged into the realms of the grey to be bothered with. You may even regard yourself as a maverick law-breaker skating the wild skateboard of freedom down the freeway of oblivion. 'Your dull rules do not apply to us, mister headteacher.'

But it is not about you …
And it is not about them …
It is about their learning.

The students in the school within which you work have various entitlements. These include the entitlement to a routine (kids thrive on routine) and to follow the same set of rules in every class, so that they are not forced into the confusing situation where they have to relearn social norms every time they move to a new lesson.

The importance of school rules as a statement of the community's shared system of values cannot be overstated. If there are 70 teachers in a school, and there is no shared vision on behaviour, then there are potentially as many as 70 different sets of rules that children have to learn. You can imagine the appalling confusion to a developing mind in this situation. If there is one set of rules, life is just easier. School becomes an easier place to learn in and an easier place in which to manage behaviour.

Imagine a room of 70 teachers.

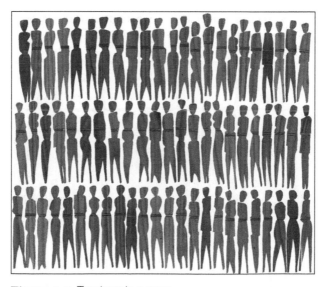

Figure 1.1 Teachers in a room

Now, imagine a long piece of rope, perhaps the biggest skipping rope you could ever possibly conceive of.

Figure 1.2 Skipping rope

The teachers are scattered around the room and all of them are holding a point of the skipping rope. They are asked to hold it as taut as possible.

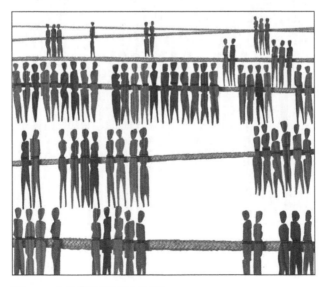

Figure 1.3 Rope in the room

What would happen if a sneaky outsider, perhaps clad in black and sporting a balaclava, snuck in and pulled down sharply on a piece of the rope?

Figure 1.4 Outsider pulling on the rope

It would create tension on the rope. At least two of the teachers, who would still be holding grimly on, might have to shift their footing a little; this may cause others to slightly shift theirs to accommodate their colleagues' change of position. But the rope would remain held by all.

This is a metaphor for the shared professional values of the staff in any school and the school policies these values mould, for example the school policy on behaviour. Any pull on it creates tension between staff.

What would happen if the same outsider used a pair of pinking shears to sever some of the rope?

When the rope is cut, some of the teachers will no longer be connected or supported and will fall over. So it is in a school. A successful staff will hold tightly on to the rules expressing shared values, recognizing that they are the invisible bonds that allow the community to function properly. If the values are disturbed by a teacher who does not understand the shared values, or by someone who is not willing to respect them, then it is possible that the whole community will suffer. The rules are the surface tension on the water on which the pond-skater is able to skate. Without this surface tension we flounder and we may drown.

Figure 1.5 Outsider with scissors

So consistency must be ensured across the school, using school policies. Students are entitled to have consistency in where they are sitting in each lesson and lessons should consistently start on time. They should have access to the resources they will need to carry out their learning and should be given clear instructions in every lesson by every teacher. Students are also entitled to consistency in the communication that they receive from all their teachers.

The five c's of compassionate communication

As a part of your professional value system as a teacher you should attempt in any communication with your students to be calm, confident, clear, compassionate and consistent.

1   *Calm* – because any other approach (particularly in respect to solving a behavioural issue) is likely to amplify a difficult situation.

2   *Confident* – because it breeds confidence. Students expect you to deal with things in the manner that might reasonably be expected of a trained and skilled professional who knows what they are doing.

3   *Clear* – because if students do not understand the instruction, then they are not going to be able to put it into action.

4   *Compassionate* – because you must care for your students' emotional landscapes, and understand that childhood – and particularly adolescence – can be a very confusing time, and that each child's starting point is different. This value must be written through your being like the word 'Blackpool' is written into a stick of seaside rock.

5   *Consistent* – because you must treat your students the same way on Monday as you would on Tuesday for the same offence. You must treat all your students the same, whether they are named Johnny or Hermione.

Everyone working together

The shared values upheld collectively by your school are the basis of the standards and expectations of your professional practice. What might appear as a collection of seemingly small things can have a significant impact, the effect of which can only be properly seen when a teacher decides unilaterally that one of them is so paltry as to be dispensed with.

Imagine please, the smallest of professional expectations – you will greet your classes at the door, every lesson, with a smile – and see it through your students' eyes. Before every lesson they are greeted politely by their name by someone who appears to like them. This practice affects and impacts upon the emotion in the building. The teachers who do this are able to monitor the behaviour in the corridors; are able to urge latecomers on, therefore affecting the punctuality to lessons; and can test the emotional temperature of the kids as they enter the room.

One teacher, however, does not think that this is worth doing.

What is the students' experience of this? Confusion. At all other lessons they are greeted at the door, but there is one teacher who does not appear to like them. There is one part of the corridor that they may fight in, or bully someone in (without anyone seeing them). There is one lesson that they do not have to get to on time. The pernicious effect of the one tiny inaction of an individual teacher permeates the building. The students who think it is okay to turn up late to this one lesson disrupt the learning in other lessons on their way to class; the students who use the opportunity of the one teacher not managing his or her bit of corridor to bully or abuse a younger child leaves another teacher to deal with the fallout.

A teacher that does not apply *all* of the shared values and school rules contributes to the potential destruction of his or her colleagues' ability to properly manage behaviour.

Managing and modelling the right behaviour within a school is first and foremost a corporate responsibility. It is the responsibility of all staff to hold the behaviour policy tight, to uphold students' rights to be in receipt of certain norms of teacher behaviour in every lesson they enter. If these norms are not held tight, then trust disappears. The behavioural guidelines are based on a joint understanding between the students and the staff, and when one side of the equation (the staff) breaks these guidelines, then students' trust is breached.

As specified earlier, to access learning straightaway students need to know what to expect: Where do I sit? Who do I work with? Do I know how I should be rewarded?

Imagine coming to work and finding that your desk had been moved without your knowledge or consent to another corner of the room. Imagine coming to work and finding that your desk is no longer there at all. How would you feel? Confused and perhaps even frightened? Imagine then how a vulnerable 11-year-old in a new school would feel if they don't know where they are sitting from lesson to lesson, or that they come into a lesson and find that you have allowed their chair to be used by someone else. Students need a framework to be free to learn. Consistency should therefore be a core part of a school's value system and is integral to implementing a successful behaviour management policy both at a whole-school level and on an individual classroom level.

Empathy

It may very well be true, that of all the human virtues kindness is the one of true lasting value. When our descendants are dead and the memories of our existence are merely the microscopic grains of sand around the long-broken statue of Ozymandias or Thatcher, our kindness may leave some atomic reverberation in the universe. It is by the existence (or not) of those acts that we should judge ourselves.

In order to be kind to our students we must become experts in the fundamental people skill of empathy. To show you why this is important, here are some statements from people who do not possess it: 'I'm not hurting the child, just showing it love.' 'This is just another form of affection.' 'This is just good discipline.' 'If she resists she's just playing hard to get.'

The child abuser, the overly brutal punitive parent and the potential rapist are all marked by their absence of empathy. If they were able to put themselves into the shoes of the person they were hurting they wouldn't do it. But they are not. Indeed the dictionary definition of a psychopath refers to empathy's absence.

The skills of empathy are often expressly described as being located in the ability to read non-verbal signals, and while this is something of a cliché, there is an element of truth to it. There is also a gender element to our ability to read non-verbal signals. As Ros Wilson, the ribald goddess of primary school literacy points out, we separate down, roughly by gender, into systematizers (males) and empathizers (females). Ask a man to read a woman's facial expression when she is, in fact, grumpy, and he will come up with a range of answers from exasperated to insane, and interestingly, will often – like a football fan hoping the replay will go in though the initial shot was saved – repeat the same suggested emotion several times in the hope that it is right the third time, though it wasn't the first and second. So, if you are a male, you may have to teach yourself to recognize emotions from facial expression and body language, as on account of your gender, you have little natural ability at this particular skill.

However, if you put yourself in the mindset of the parents of the students you are teaching, then, above all, they would want you to be kind to them. In addition, they would want you to be empathetic: to have compassion for their child's tribulations.

There are skills you can develop in this area. One of which is to mirror the body language of the child you are talking to. This goes back to Freud. In studying a series of people who counselled and psychoanalysed, he came to the conclusion that those who were best able to empathize with their patients were those who were subtly able to inhabit the body language of the people they were working with. It is entirely possible to carry out a related exper-iment in the comfort of your own home. Ask someone you live with to write down ten emotions and to then perform the facial expressions that accompany the first five of these. Attempt to guess them. Ask them to perform the next five, but before you try to guess you must mirror their expression back to them. Generally, people find it easier to recognize the emotion being shown to them if they inhabit its facial and body expression first.

How, being in possession of this information, do you use it in a classroom situation? Mirroring a crying child by crying yourself could be regarded as being overempathetic! The answer is that you must employ this technique subtly and you must do so predominantly with your body. If a child's shoulders are slumped over, then you slump yours; if their head is hung low, you do the same. You stay in that position for a while before you talk to them and you will find that, in aligning yourself with their body language, you are better able to empathize with them. Moreover, it is easier for them to communicate with you, as you are on their level.

Fairness

The children in your classroom are individuals with individual rights. It is a mistake made by a first term's Newly Qualified Teacher (NQT) to dole out punishments to a whole class because 29 out of the 30 have been misbehaving. Put yourself in the shoes of the spindly boy with the cowlick who is obsessed with dinosaurs, and has done nothing wrong whatsoever, but is suffering because of the behaviour of others. The first principle of fairness is that group punishments do not work and should not be applied. The second is that you must judge each interaction on its own merits: the fact that the child involved in a particular incident was naughty yesterday or has a reputation for naughtiness should not affect your judgement. The third is, in dealing with behaviour, you should not rely on position or status; you should deal rationally with the incident in question. You might well feel like saying, 'Because I said so, right?' or, 'Because I am the teacher, and what I say goes', but it is not best practice. While you should not get into huge negotiations with someone who is misbehaving, and also acknowledging that teachers are the bottom line in the classroom, it is not unreasonable for a confused child to expect a rational explanation of your decisions.

What happens when things go wrong?

In the real world, of course, things do go wrong. A teacher will accidentally (or deliberately) allow that core set of values to be broken: allow the rope to be cut. In the real world, the solution to this is simple: you restore trust.

Apologize if you make a mistake. Students need to know you are, like them, a human being, flawed perhaps, like all of us, but ostensibly the same animal as them. As the adult you are supposed to be modelling the behaviour you expect from them, and you would expect an apology if they had made a mistake. In saying sorry for something that you have done wrong, you not only model the behaviour you want to see, but you repair the rope: you reinstate the value system.

Test yourself

As we specified in the introduction, at the end of this and every chapter, we will ask you to fill in the relevant section of the questionnaire again to evaluate your new understanding and what you have learnt. There may still be areas in which you feel under-confident, and that what this chapter has done is to prick your interest in that area, revealing, perhaps, that you need to do further research in order to become confident. Be aware that, often, your best friend is time and experience. It is possible that an area you have identified as a 'development need' will be a skill that you develop naturally over time.

	Very confident	Confident	Not confident	Huh?
Are you who you should be internally?				
I am aware of my own value system.				
I know all the school rules on behaviour.				
I implement all the school rules on behaviour.				
I am consistent, and treat each situation on its particular merits.				

I display empathy easily.				
I am fair.				

Chapter 2
Can you manage your own behaviour?

Circles of transmission and receipt – Betari's Box

In communicating with a new class you are in a circle of transmission and receipt: both you and the class are transmitting and receiving verbal and non-verbal information. The Betari's Box (Figure 2.1) is a simple circular diagram that shows how attitude and behaviour are linked.

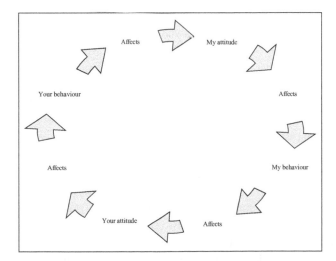

Figure 2.1 Betari's Box

Your attitude affects your behaviour

In their seminal, though controversial work, *Pygmalion in the Classroom – Teacher Expectation and Pupils' Intellectual Development*, Robert Rosenthal and Leonore Jacobson ask you to imagine two scenarios, which can be used to examine how attitude in certain situations affects behaviour.

Scenario 1: Imagine you are meeting someone for the first time, who you only know of by reputation; let's call him Peter. Now, Peter is known for being exceptionally clever, but his intellect is reputedly used for foul means rather than fair: he is rumoured to enjoy making other people feel stupid by comparison. Peter is a member of the senior management team in a place of learning, and is known, behind his back, as 'the smiling assassin'. You also have a particularly good reason to dislike Peter. When a very dear friend of yours, someone whom you love, respect and admire, was undergoing a devastating personal trauma she approached Peter asking for some respite and understanding at work. Not only was it not given, but Peter took your friend's weakness as an excuse to load more and more work upon her. Imagine meeting Peter for the first time. Imagine shaking his hand!

How would your prior knowledge of Peter affect your body language?

What signals would you give away?

Most likely you would be starchy in your approach: your smile, should it exist, would be unconvincing and you might arch your upper body away from him. You would be transmitting signals of distrust and, interestingly, if you acknowledge that humans often mirror the behaviour that they witness in others, you would probably be creating the conditions for Peter to be dislikeable, as he would be highly likely to mirror your body language. Similarly, it would affect your language: you would watch every word that you said, and would go to that first meeting with the firm consciousness to assert yourself, and probably thinking that you wouldn't leave the room having agreed to anything.

Scenario 2: Now imagine meeting someone else; Sarah. Again, you only know this person by reputation, and that reputation is for being very clever indeed. However, unlike Peter, the only real way that people know Sarah is clever is because she has an incisively wicked sense of humour. The moment Sarah's name is mentioned you have noticed that people light up: everybody you know likes Sarah. You also have it on good authority that Sarah is a truly great person, because when a very dear friend of yours, whom you love, respect and admire, was undergoing a devastating personal trauma and was in a medieval emotional landscape Sarah not only held her up by the elbow for a full 18 months forcing her to put one foot in front of the other, but she also told her spine-splittingly funny gags while she was doing it.

Imagine meeting Sarah for the first time and shaking her hand!

How would your prior knowledge affect your body language? What signals would you give away?

You probably wouldn't be able to contain your delight and excitement about meeting someone so nice; you may even find the urge to cuddle her almost irresistible!

In exactly the same manner as when we expect to dislike someone, going into a situation expecting to like someone creates the conditions for them to be likeable. Your body language here will be warm, open and effusive; your facial expression gleeful and interested, and your tone of voice upbeat, excited and positive. As a result, these attitudes would, in all probability, be reflected back to you.[1]

You may think you are good at putting up a pretence, but whatever attitude you have about a situation you are unconsciously seeping out through external displays. The signals that you transmit through facial expressions, body language, tone of voice, and also even the words you use, are massively affected by your attitude to that situation.

Both authors are often plunged into professional situations where they have to form relationships very quickly. When Phil visits a school to work with a group of kids in Manchester, or Stoke, or Corby (or wherever), he is often advised that the students are likely to be difficult, and that two in particular are very challenging. What the teacher doesn't realize is that it is their own limiting judgement that is making the student difficult to manage (for that teacher). As a matter of policy Phil chooses to ignore this judgment and to expect the students in question to be delightful and charming. And guess what?!...

Something else to remember is that all human relationships have the capacity for permanent breakdown. Going into a class with an awareness of

---

[1] Unless, of course, you go completely over the top and come across as a prize idiot. Both these scenarios are a pastiche of a section in the quite brilliant *Pygmalion in the Classroom* (Rosenthal and Jacobson, 1992).

this, combined with the recognition that every relationship that is conducted in a classroom has to be nurtured, is vital. Without a nurtured and deeply held understanding of this you may not even manage to strike up the relationship, and you certainly won't be able to retain it.

So, the first thing you need to get right, when entering a difficult class or a challenging school is your attitude to the situation. If you go into a class with a fearful attitude, then this is likely to transmit to your audience, as you'll behave in a fearful manner. If, on the other hand, you enter the environment determined to recognize the good in everyone, committed to the service of your students' education and prepared to ensure that every situation that plays out will be treated in a positive and professional manner, then you are halfway there.

Your behaviour affects their attitude

A teacher who wants to have a happy, orderly class must embody the behaviour they want their students to reflect back.

Moreover, you should have a consciousness that whatever signals you send out, inevitably, as this is the nature of human social contact, have an effect on the attitude of the people receiving those signals. Here it is a case of being observant and analytical about the behaviours you display in a classroom environment, and what their effect appears to be on the attitude of your students: you must be a 'reflective practitioner'.

There is the complicating issue that your students are individuals and they will (probably, though not necessarily) have individual responses to your behaviour: what one student might regard as endearingly madcap behaviour from the teacher, another will regard as empirical evidence that the teacher is certifiably insane. You must therefore be observant of how your behaviour affects their attitude, individually, as well as on a whole-class level.

To exemplify this sensitivity, below are the descriptions of five Year 11 students who Phil taught, and how each individual personality had to be managed.

Agnetha is a charming, intelligent student, in what appears to be quite an adult relationship with Eric. She has been demoted from the top set for lack of work, is of very high academic ability for the inner cities and dresses in a slightly oversexualized manner.

Eric is Agnetha's boyfriend. Again, he is bright and charming, capable of high order and original analysis, though this sometimes does not translate to his written work. The fact that he is (currently) Agnetha's boyfriend appears to be the focal point of his existence.

Kareem blithely and relatively happily inhabits the role of class clown, though he is not disruptive in any way. He is overweight and makes light of this, constantly being the butt of banter, which, despite its potential hurtfulness, does not appear to have any edge of nastiness.

Simon has recently been excluded from another school, and came to this school from a Pupil Referral Unit. He has a reputation for misbehaviour and lack of focus throughout the school, and is certainly a little over laconic in English lessons. But he smiles readily and is – almost – aware that he has some talent in the subject.

David is a very quiet Filipino boy. He is the victim of some bullying despite his physical solidity and he appears to be very focused on academic attainment.

With each of these students, as with every student you will ever encounter, there are individual nuances that a skilled teacher should take into account during every interaction. When dealing with Eric and Agnetha, it was important to be respectful of their relationship, while at the same time not letting any behaviour that was inappropriate for a classroom spill over into lessons. Both students also required consistent affirmation that they were every bit as intelligent as they suspected themselves to be, Eric more so than Agnetha. Importantly, given Agnetha's penchant for revealing attire, the teacher always had to place himself in a position relative to her, so that her 'displays' were not evident to his eye from that angle.

With Kareem, it was necessary to act as a protector if the playful ribbing ever began to border on damaging, and to ensure he was aware that he did not have to tolerate abuse. Simon was allowed the odd laconic day, and before challenging him about his work it helped to engage him in gentle joking about his work-rate. David required concrete and detailed marking and for praise to be given in private, preferably in written form. It was important to let David know that his teacher recognized that David knew what he was at school for, and that they would work together as a team to achieve the grades he wanted.

Your behaviour towards your students needs to be differentiated and personalized, and you have to be analytical about it. With one of these students, Kareem, Phil committed an error of judgement in terms of his own behaviour, doing something in jest that caused the student to think that he was insane (and not in a good way) that required remedial work over the space of a month to win back the student's trust. Trust is pivotal. It takes you a long time to win it, and it can be easily thrown away; but if it is, you simply retie the rope: reinstate the trust by behaving in a manner that would make a student regard you as trustworthy again.

The students' attitude affects their behaviour

A student's attitude to a situation will, of course, affect their behaviour too. You may behave completely professionally but still find yourself at the mercy of a collectively unconscious decision by a class that their new teacher is not likeable, and is therefore not to be liked. It can be brutal being at the mercy of this decision, particularly when it appears, at the time, that it is an opinion to which the whole class subscribes. But this mob behaviour will eventually play out, as you pick off their erroneous opinions of you, one child at a time. You can do this by ensuring that in every individual inter-action you are as utterly nice and as utterly supportive as you would want your own children's teachers to be. A negative opinion of you will not persist if it is manifestly and demonstrably based on falsehood.

However, at this stage it is possible that you can find yourself in a spiral of faulty communication that can get completely out of control. If you think about the nature of communication with any decent analytical sensibility, then you can determine that, basically, it boils down to transmission and receipt. You may transmit enthusiasm and liking, but it can be received by a class who are stuck in a state of manipulative aggression to be an expression of negativity. What you transmit is not necessarily what is received.

At this point of the transaction the temptation, when you are in receipt of what feels like a barrage or a tidal wave of negativity, is to reflect that negativity back. This is understandable, but it is not the response of a skilled professional: in reflecting back negative attitudes and behaviours you are merely amplifying them and confirming to your class that their feeling about you was right – you do not like them. It is permissible, though unpalatable, for a class to be faulty receivers and it is permissible for them to receive your good intentions and your liking of them as its opposite. What is not permissible is for a trained professional teacher to be a faulty transmitter whose transmission gives any credence to a class's claims that you do not like them. If that is the case then you are allowing their behaviour to affect your attitude, which is the cardinal sin of managing behaviour in challenging schools.

The students' behaviour affects your attitude

You will be in a constant internal dialogue, attempting to assess and judge the behaviour of the class, what it is signalling to you and what you can do about it. What can often happen at this stage is that teacher and class can get into a subconscious loop of faulty transmission and receipt: you go into the classroom fearful and anxious and behave in a manner that subconsciously transmits this anxiety; this is received as weakness or anger by the students and if affects their attitude towards you. They misbehave. You go into the next lesson even more anxious, even more fearful. An escalating ballet stuck in a time warp.

It is at this stage where being a professional comes into play. It is at this stage that we can break the cycle.

Do not let their behaviour affect your attitude!

To change students' behaviour your first step is to be aware of your own attitudes, and how they are inclined to affect your own behaviour, and then how your behaviour affects other people, specifically your students. In the meantime, before you have managed to change their bad behaviour, you can ensure your attitude is not affected by their behaviour by recording on paper how the behaviour of the class, or of individuals within the class, makes you feel and, from there, make a stand that you will refuse to let it affect your attitude.

If you don't do this you will be stuck in the circle of faulty transmission and receipt, which merely escalates issues: the child/class transmits anger, you reflect it, it all spirals. It is the teachers' professional responsibility to the class and to their own sanity to reverse what is being transmitted: they transmit anger, you transmit compassion and warmth. In doing so, you break the amplifying effect of the loop.

You may feel at this point that you are being forced into a situation in which you are required to be submissive to a group of children. This is an understandable, though incorrect perception: what you are doing is adopting a trained, professional response. You are the one in control – it just might not feel like it for a bit.

It is at this point that a concerned professional, who is determined to get on top of things behaviourally, will conduct a 'behaviour impact analysis', both on themselves and on the behaviour of the class.[2] With a particularly difficult class you may want to do this on a nightly basis until you have it cracked.

Behaviour Impact Analysis (BIA)

To successfully confront the challenging behaviour of others you must first examine your own challenging behaviour(s). It is in modelling an ability to change to your classes that you can begin to model the behaviour you want to see. You can do this by being honest with yourself about what your own challenging behaviours are, about the impact those behaviours have upon others and their level of acceptability. Having done this you can look for solutions. (You can change.)

Here is an analysis of some of Phil's incidences of poor behaviour in the domestic sphere. (They are legion.)

- Not putting the clean clothes away in the kids' wardrobes but just piling them neatly on the downstairs table, expecting someone else (my wife) to finish the job.

- Overworking, then becoming fed up and feeling as if I never have any fun.

- Being compulsive and hasty, making snap decisions without thinking the consequences through.

- Worrying, particularly about money and the future.

- Compulsively overworking.

---

[2] Whether you share the results of the BIA on the class with the class is an interesting question that we will leave to your professional discretion.

Having identified these challenging behaviours, their effect and level of acceptability can be discussed with the person on whom they most impact – in this case Mrs Beadle. The responses she made are as truthful as she could manage without precipitating Phil into full nervous breakdown! Her answers are in the second and third column of the table below. The fourth column details the changes that have occurred (or not) as a result of the behaviour impact analysis.

Behaviour	Impact on the other	Acceptability?	Change?
Not putting the clean clothes away in the kids' cupboards but just piling them neatly on the downstairs table.	'It has to be done so I just zen out and do it.'	'Not acceptable, but I accept it.'	I put the washing away now.
Overworking, then becoming fed up and feeling as if I never have any fun.	'I attempt to rationalize, sympathize and calm you … and I do sympathize, genuinely, but …'	'It is totally unacceptable. You must change this. It is a monologue. Your fatalism and resignation to this is unnecessary.'	I do not accept every offer of work. (In theory, anyway.)
Being compulsive and hasty, making snap decisions without thinking the consequences through.	'Irritation. As the decision has already been made without my input, then the only option I have is to criticize.'	'Unacceptable.'	There have been episodes of hasty decision-making. They have had negative results.

Worrying, particularly about money and the future.	'I block this out. Worrying is bad for you, as it can turn into panic, and any decision made in a state of panic cannot be good.'	'Not really acceptable.'	I'm a worrier.
Compulsively overworking	'I tend to regard this as a gender stipulation. It's related to your version of masculinity.	'It's not acceptable, as it's compulsive.'	This book has been delivered substantially later than expected.

The fascinating element of doing an exercise such as this is that some of the things (and let's relocate this to the classroom) that you may regard as strengths may be perceived by others as being unacceptable. For instance, while 'worrying' could be regarded as being the trigger to long-term planning by the worrier, it could also be thought of as 'unacceptable' by someone else. Unless we investigate the impact of our behaviour on others, we don't really know it; we don't own it.

What behaviours do you masquerade as strengths that could actually be having a substantially negative impact on your students?

Do your own professional version of a BIA. Identify your own behavioural issues in the classroom – are you prone to shouting, for instance; do you talk too much about how fantastic you are? Then analyse the impact of these on others (in this case your students), their level of acceptability and what you are able to do (if anything) to change your behaviour. Scottish blogger and head of English, N. Winton, in his markedly open-hearted blog, 'If You Don't Like Change … You're Going to Like Irrelevance Even Less' argues that, 'Everything starts with the learner' and leads educators to ask themselves a series of probing questions, which may well be of use when you are analysing your own classroom behaviour:

- Would you want to be taught by you? What do you do that would annoy you?

- Do you annoy the class in any way because of what you do?

- If you are confrontational with anyone in the class, what are the rest of the class thinking? What would you be thinking if you were another learner in the class?

- Are your lessons engaging for the learners? Do they want to learn? Do they do the bare minimum, or do they ever want to do more?

- When did you last ask anyone in one of your classes what they enjoyed doing?[3]

He also observes that, 'We are reluctant to consider questions that we already know will give negative answers.' But it is vital that, as a teacher who wants to be the best teacher they can be in a challenging environment, that you are able to face up to analysing yourself and asking yourself unpalatable questions about your own behaviour. You can be pretty sure that your classes are going to ask you these questions in time, and it is sensible to already have the answers prepared. So get going on an analysis of your own behaviour and, from there, you can start modelling the ability to change.

You might then choose to do the same exercise with the behaviour of the class. List incidents of bad behaviour that have happened in your lessons, examine their impact on the learning, then assess their acceptability or not, and look at possible changes that can be made. It may be that this information performs the useful function of starting a scaffolded circle-time style discussion of your analysis in which you examine with your class the acceptability or not of various examples of poor behaviour and what can be done to change it. More bravely, it could be that you use the impact analysis of your own behaviour to be the prompt for the discussion; in sharing this with your class you will be modelling what you want to see from them: honesty about the results of their behaviour in class, and an analytical approach to the impact of their behaviour.

Managing relationships

Anthropologically, British schools would be as strange to a visiting alien as our habit of standing at a busy bar waving a tenner at an overworked barmaid genuinely expecting her to serve us more quickly than the poor sap

---

[3] http://nwinton.wordpress.com/

who is only holding out a fiver might be to a visiting Frenchman. Schools are environments in which the most exciting teacher may well be the one who takes the most risks; but they are also environments where adherence to a code must run up against a teacher's sense of their own individuality without there being too much friction. It is possible for you to adhere to the expected code of teacher behaviour without it impinging too far on your own sense of self, or your own particular notion of teaching brilliance. Let us look at the varying categories of relationship that can occur within a school:

1   Staff with staff
2   Staff with pupils
3   Pupils with pupils
4   Staff with parents

With the exception of the third category, which is a variety of relationship you are not directly involved in, your core professional standards and practice will require you to adhere to certain norms in each of these areas.

Staff with staff

If you let your colleagues down, then you are contributing to another tiny snip of the invisible bonds that keep the community stable. If you are late and have to ring in, another teacher will have to cover the first ten minutes of your lesson when they could have been marking a book or planning a lesson. Your lateness will not only affect the learning and achievement of the children you are paid to teach, but it will put your colleague under stress.

So turn up, and turn up on time. If you get into a habit of turning up late or bunking off, you are – to use a phrase once coined by an ex-colleague 'Robbing off your colleagues.'[4] If you do find yourself being unavoidably late at any time, make sure you ring in the moment you realize and give the school office a reasonable idea of what time you are going to arrive. It is one thing being late; it is entirely another being late and no one knowing about it.

Your colleagues are your support network in good times and in bad, and it is vitally important to your ability to manage behaviour that you are a 'good' colleague. If you are not, it may be that the senior manager whose

---

[4] Which is outrageously harsh ... until you think about it.

help you desperately need in a dire situation will find themselves inclined to tardiness. What goes around comes around.

You will form two kinds of relationships with your colleagues: bridging and bonding. Bonding relationships are those with a deep involvement; they are nourishing, but you cannot have too many of them, otherwise you will not be able to service them. Bridging relationships are more functional; they are about getting something done on the day.

Varieties of relationships with staff

There are at least five different varieties of staff-on-staff relationships you will have: your trusted mates (bonding relationships), your colleagues (bridging), your bosses (bridging), any learning support assistants or teachers you work with (bridging) and, finally, ancillary staff (bridging).

First off, talk with your mates how you want to talk – just be careful who's listening! But communication with all other members of staff, of whatever variety, has to run along professional lines. Remember you are focused on the learning of your students, and of all the students in the whole community, and any conversations with colleagues should be conducted with this focus in mind.

The key when you are talking to another member of staff is remaining calm in all situations. There are times when you are working in challenging schools that your temperament will be tested to its limits. It is okay to express exasperation, but if you are talking to anyone other than a dear, trusted friend then this has to be in professional language and, above all, you must model the kind of behaviour you want to see in your students. This is not to say that you cannot reveal an extant emotional life, but do your best not to lose it with a colleague! In a professional dialogue keep a gimlet-eyed focus on the achievement of your students, and what the best path in any given situation is for them, and you will not go far wrong.

(A word on teachers and emotional outbursts. You are in luck that you have entered a profession that is predominantly populated by extremely nice people. However, if you find yourself being pushed to the emotional limit by behaviour so much that you burst into tears in the presence of another adult, do not beat yourself up about it. It is an emotional experience teaching in a challenging school and dealing with children who may be from desperate backgrounds, and it is highly likely that the person you are crying in front of has been in the same situation themselves and is entirely able to empathize with your situation. While it is not a strategy that you will want to get a reputation for, it happens: professional people cry too. You will usually find that the colleague who you feel you are humiliating yourself in front of will be utterly kind and utterly supportive).

Relationships with non-teaching staff

These must be respectful, and can be cheery. Be aware that, just as the health of any society may reasonably be judged by the treatment of its most vulnerable members, your worth as a teacher and as a human being is related to your treatment of the lowest paid people in the building. If you give any sense that you are better than your colleagues, you are not the kind of person who should be given the gift of spending their time around the developing passions and interests of young people! 'Nuff said: be nice.

Staff with pupils

In terms of the coverage of this book this variety of relationship is obviously the pivotal one, and it is what the majority of the book covers. Consequently, a discrete section of this chapter covering how to properly manage the relationships between staff and students would take in the region of 50,000 words under a subheading, and would make for a difficult read.

What we will cover here are a few challenging behaviours that you might be inclined to manifest, and why you should control yourself in these areas.

Can't shout: won't shout

This is a mildly, though progressively less, controversial area. Fifteen years ago there was a sense in the profession that it was okay, absolutely fine even, to express your anger at a student, and to do so in a very loud tone of voice. Now, however, the reverse is frequently the case. There is even a temptation among some management teams to adopt the not-shouting approach unquestioningly, almost as a form of religion, or as a credo which infers moral superiority.

It is worth bearing in mind both sides of the argument. Here from Old Andrew, the consistently entertaining and analytical blogger behind the outrageously well-argued blog 'Scenes from the Battleground' is an interesting thought piece about how not shouting has become a badge of moral purity.

Recently, I have seen the disapproval of shouting take the same tone as the opponents of corporal punishment took, that of complete and unquestioning disapproval from a position of moral superiority, unsupported by a rational argument. It's put me in a bit of a dilemma. I have worked in both 'shouting schools' and 'no shouting schools' and have preferred the latter. I trained in a school with an explicit no shouting policy and actually rather enjoyed it. When I worked at the Metropolitan School the students were savvy enough to know that forcing a teacher to shout at the class would be a sure sign that they had got to them, and, therefore, raising your voice in class would just make kids laugh at you. The discipline system there had clear sanctions, which did not include taking a kid out and shouting at them. Therefore, there was very little point to shouting at all. Even when I have worked in a 'shouting school', I would try hard to avoid shouting at classes; it was a high-risk strategy and I was experienced enough at managing classes to know how to deal with noise in a more structured and careful way. Therefore, I have no particular support for shouting, and little reason to advocate it as a form of behaviour management.[5]

Teachers have come to the realization that it's horrible being shouted at and, fairly importantly, it doesn't work. Shouting at anyone on a one-to-one basis is an idiot's strategy. It is hurtful, frightening and is a pathetically ineffective way of communicating anything other than the fact that you have completely lost it! If you want to communicate with an individual, then speak to them. And, more importantly, listen to what they have to say!

Where it is more of a grey area is in a whole-class situation. Where the class behaviour or, more likely, the noise level and off-task talk has got to a point where you are pretty certain that absolutely nothing of any task-related consequence is going on, then the temptation will be to shout, to take one decisive piece of amplified throat action, in order to regain control of a situation. It does work, and as it works, there is, quite obviously, the temptation to use it as a strategy.

However, there are better ways of managing the situation than shouting. Counting down from three to one is something we have seen work (most of the time). Holding the hand up and expecting every student to hold their

---

[5] http://teachingbattleground.wordpress.com/

hand up and to shush at the same time can work too. With these techniques, though, there has to be an element of buy-in first, and then of drilling and persistence to keep them going. Otherwise, you can get into fruitlessly intoning the negative hundreds with the counting exercise, or just standing with your hand up in a room for an hour while a riot rages around you.

Do not discuss confidential business in front of a student

This shouldn't need stating, but for some reason there are a few people who do not quite understand that discussing the conduct of either a colleague or a student in front of another student is unprofessional and will cause pupils to lose respect for you. Teaching is a profession, and there are expectations that come with that nomenclature. Students prefer teachers who do not discuss the work of a colleague in front of, or with, them. They dislike it when you bad mouth a colleague. They wonder why teachers do it, and why teachers are so competitive with each other. Behave like an adult. It is what you are meant to be.

Try not to swear

Using sexual swear words as even an exclamation can have you sacked and you do not want to get a reputation for being out of control of any aspect of your behaviour.

In addition, any discriminatory comment should be avoided like a rabid dog. You are not to be abusive in any way in terms of your language to any of the children you teach.

Don't put temptation in anyone's way

Imagine that you are from a family with little in the way of material provision and possession of an iPhone is seen as the ultimate status symbol. The teacher has left her bag open on the desk, at the top of which is a shiny new iPhone. You don't generally steal, but, you know, it's an iPhone. With the help of a paperclip and an instructional video from YouTube, it could be your iPhone. It would have been much easier if the teacher hadn't left her bag open, just begging for the iPhone to be stolen.

'Oh, her purse is there too! I won't get into trouble if I don't get caught.'

Staff with parents

Early communication with parents is a very useful path to take when you are managing a class in a challenging situation. In fact, it can be the quickest and surest way of gaining control of the behaviour of a challenging child. What you must establish very early on is the fact that you will follow through with whatever reward or consequence that has been identified as appropriate for unacceptable behaviour.

For students, the 'phone call home' is often seen as the nuclear sanction. If you put yourself in the shoes of the parent, and imagine having a teacher ringing them up or, better still, sending them a letter informing them that the behaviour of their beloved offspring is in the vicinity of unacceptable, you can imagine what that parent's response might be: they would most likely go cataclysmic. The transient teacher/student relationship and the permanent parent/child relationship are nowhere near the same thing, and you will find the student who is utterly disrespectful of your authority as a teacher will be rightly petrified of any negative emotion being expressed by their parent(s).

A phenomenally successful idea is to phone parents up at an early stage to congratulate them on the behaviour, or attainment, of their child. By getting in first and establishing a rapport in the good times, then it becomes permissible that, in less good times, the relationship can be leant on.

Positive first. Reward first.

When it comes to contacting parents and informing them that their child's behaviour has gone in the direction of naughty, most teachers reach quickly in the direction of the mobile phone. There are reasons, though, that written communication is a more reliable and successful means of communication. First, it gives the parents evidence of their child's misdemeanours that they can point to when they are upbraiding – there is no denying them, and secondly you can be exact: the cataloguing of the behaviour in written form allows you to record the manifestations of unacceptable that have occurred during the lesson.

And there is no pointless dialogue.

If you do decide to phone the parents, you must start with the positive first. Say two positive things about their child, for example, their intelligence, the fact that they have previously made a good start to lessons, or mention a specific piece of work that they have done well. Then you should detail the bad behaviour and ask the parent to 'have a gentle word' about what is acceptable behaviour for learning. It may be that this will be the only time that you have to speak to the parent, or it may be that it is the first part of a long dialogue, but it is key that you remain positive and focused on the child's well-being and attainment, and that it is demonstrably obvious to the parent that you have the best interest of their child and their child's learning at heart. Needless to say, you must conduct yourself in a professional and respectful manner in any communication with parents.

Should parents express anger at any point during the conversation, then a useful approach is to say: 'I am going to listen to you, and I need to know what the issues are and what you would like me to do.' You will find that, since all parents have been to school, and many may have had negative experiences during their education, they are carrying a lot of baggage. Using the above line will tend to negate their preconceived opinions of teachers.

Parents' evenings

There are very few formal points of contact between parents and teachers over the space of the school year; the chief one, of course, is the parents' evening. This happens once a year for each year group, and you can pretty well guarantee that the students' parents whom you most want to see in order to have a firm chat about behaviour will be absent (which tells a story): either they are not sufficiently interested in their children's education to have any real involvement and, by implication, endorse their child's unacceptable behaviour in the classroom, or – as is often the case with single parents – they are desperately struggling to keep up with things financially and are having to work evenings, leaving their kids either unsupervised or in the care of someone else for long periods.

When parents do turn up at a parents' evening, there is a chief sin that teachers often commit which you should avoid. Whatever you do, don't launch into a lengthy disquisition where you start going on about the fact that Dave or Albert is a nice boy. This is not the realm of the professional, and if you talk nonsense, like how sweet a child is or what a lovely smile he or she has, then a parent with half a brain will identify, quite correctly, that you are a tad too daft to be a teacher.

What you should convey to the parents is how well their child is doing in the subject, what level he or she is at, and exactly and technically what he or she needs to do to improve at the subject. A proper professional would have their rigorously marked books available for inspection and would show the parents exactly what the student has achieved and where there are areas for improvement.

Where there are behavioural issues with the young person whose parents are in front of you, then you must cover them briskly and professionally. Do not be apologetic: it is not you who has anything to apologize for, and do not stint on your description of the behaviour and its impact on everyone in the room. It is possible, though unlikely, that you will be in receipt of every teacher's worst nightmare: the angry parent. Then you must employ whatever de-escalation techniques you are able to muster (see Chapter 6), and you must refer the parent to whoever is the most senior member of the management team available. It is their job to deal with it. They are paid more than you, and one of the reasons they are paid more than you is that they have to defuse the angry parents.

Another useful tip in terms of your conduct at parents' evenings is not to make any stupid assumptions about social class and value systems on the basis of appearance, or on the basis of the child's behaviour. Often a child's parenting or background will not be immediately evident from their conduct in school. You may assume that you are talking to an unemployed truck driver, and will adjust your register accordingly, only to find out that the parent of the utterly disaffected student is, in fact, a defrocked Oxford don. Don't assume as, to quote *Carry on Screaming*, 'You make an ASS out of U and ME.'

Test yourself

	Very confident	Confident	Not confident	Huh?
Can you manage your own behaviour?				
I can analyse cycles of transmission and receipt.				

I am aware that my attitude affects my behaviour.				
I differentiate my behaviour for different students.				
I can break a faulty circle of transmission and receipt.				
I can conduct a behaviour impact analysis.				
I am aware of the full varieties of relationship that I will have to manage.				
I know why I shouldn't shout.				
I know why I shouldn't discuss confidential business in front of students.				
I know the differences between bonding and bridging relationships.				

Chapter 3
Are you who you should be externally?

Albert Mehrabian and conveying 'liking'

The work of Albert Mehrabian, an Armenian psychologist, is responsible for an area of study that has had a substantial impact on the way we view behaviour management.

He conducted a series of experiments around what it is that influences whether we like someone or not. His first experiment was to ask people to listen to a series of female voices saying the word 'Maybe' in three separate tones: first, in a tone that might be taken to convey liking, then in a neutral tone and, finally, in a tone intended to convey disliking. They were then shown pictures of female faces displaying expressions intended to show liking, neutrality and dislike. They listened to the tape in isolation, were shown the pictures in isolation and were then asked to listen to the tape and view the pictures in combination.

The data from this experiment led Mehrabian to the conclusion that people are more able to discern whether they are liked, disliked, or are the object of ambivalence from the expression on a face than they are from the tone in a voice.

Mehrabian's second experiment was to have nine different words recorded in varying tones of voice. The words themselves had an association with either liking ('honey', 'dear' and 'thanks'); neutrality ('may', 'really' and 'oh'); or disliking ('don't', 'brute' and 'terrible'). It was found that the tone in which the words were said was a more reliable indicator of recognizing the emotion than the actual meaning of the words.

These experiments led Mehrabian to construct an (in no way uncontroversial) formula:

Total liking = 7% Verbal liking + 38% Vocal liking + 55% Facial liking[1]

In other words, we make decisions as to whether someone likes us predominantly on the basis of their facial expression and the tone of their voice: what is actually said is accountable for only a small part of communicating liking.

In terms of the breakdown between the effectiveness of various forms of communication, non-verbal signals account for over half of the effectiveness (or not) of the communication. Over half of your ability to influence any given situation occurs before you have even gone so far as to open your mouth. And of the percentage that is verbal, most of this is reliant on the tone of voice you employ. If we are in a situation with someone we have no existing relationship of trust with – a new teacher, for instance – then we are inclined to pay substantially more attention to what we hear and what we see than to what they might say.

How then to manipulate how you come across to your students so that they begin to trust you as quickly as is possible? What non-verbal devices can be used to elicit trust at an early stage?

Liking – the importance of facial expression

American writer and political activist Max Eastman is credited with the phrase, 'Dogs laugh with their tails. What puts man in a higher state of evolution is that he has got his laugh on the right end.'[2] If we acknowledge Mehrabian, there is much that can be achieved in the classroom with what Eastman describes as the 'Universal welcome'[3]: the smile.

When you smile at a baby, what does it do? It smiles back. When you smile at an ape, it does the same. Animal behaviourists at the University of

---

[1] Meharabian, 1971.
[2] Eastman, 1939.
[3] Eastman, 1939.

Plymouth have identified that chimpanzees as young as one-month-old are able to smile and to laugh, and that they will respond in kind to a human smile.[4]

Primates have a gene that, from an early age, aids us in mimicking the behaviour of those around us. Why? Because being able to copy or mimic is a vital developmental tool for learning the skills that will keep us alive. (In addition, it could be argued this ability is there to make us engaging. In smiling back at our mother we engage her hormones so she continues to dote on us, and therefore to protect us.) Scientists' best guesses as to the evolution of laughter are that it originated as a response to a threatening situation that doesn't actually end in the pain we anticipated. Neuroscientist V. S. Ramachandran has identified that the pain, fear and laughter pathways are 'intimately interconnected',[5] and it is postulated that the heaving grimace of the laughing face is merely a relaxed version of the grimace of fear. Laughter is, therefore, the ultimate expression of safety.

Arguably, it is the existence of the mirror gene that contributes to the viral nature of emotion. Whatever the root of this reality, possession of this piece of knowledge should aid you in your path towards managing the class. You set the mood: what you give out is – in most cases – what you will get back. Laugh and you will set a mood; scowl and you will do the same. It is, therefore, vital that you model the behaviour that you wish the class to adopt.

To illustrate the importance of getting your behaviour right and keeping the rictus grin on your face, here are a couple of stories based on one of the author's experiences.

Phil had been assigned to mentor a very talented and unbelievably hard-working maths teacher who was having a few issues with classroom control. He was a great teacher and a delightful human being, but the kids couldn't stand him, and quite reasonably, as he was a lovely man, he was somewhat confused by their reaction. 'Phil, why do they hate me so much?' he exclaimed in frustration, palm flat against his forehead. 'Well,' replied Phil, 'I think the answer here is quite simple … it is probably because you are hateful.'

Despite the fact that in all other areas he was a lovely man, clearly a

---

[4] Carr and Greeves, 2007, p. 18.
[5] Carr and Greeves, 2007, p. 21.

wonderful and gentle father and an utterly dedicated professional, he was so worried about discipline, and had been told so many times by well-meaning idiots not to smile before Christmas that he was not at all likeable in class. He shouted, was overly cross and overly punitive. Sure enough, the aggression he gave out was reflected back at him. As one of the kids said, 'Look sir/man. If you go "Rah" in the mirror, what does it do? It goes "Rah" back at you.'

Phil also worked with another beautiful human when, during his twenties, he found himself treading water working in a major bank which he won't name (it was the Abbey National) on a very boring project. The project was staffed with about 150 people, and if you mentioned the name of this one person, who he won't name, to any person in the building they would immediately start beaming and say, 'Oh, Denis, I love him. Isn't he great?' There was not a single person in the building who was not prepared to launch into paroxysms of atomic wonder at the mere thought of his face. Every clerk in the building thought they had a very special relationship with Denis; scratch any one of them and you would find that they would all have, 'I love Denis' written through their bone marrow.

This confused Phil. As a committed and certified iconoclast, even at such an early age, he had resolved not to like the sainted Denis, on the basis that if everyone else is blindly agreeing that something is right then it is surely wrong (and liking Denis was the default setting of everyone in the building). But it was impossible. For Denis, unlike many others in the building, was intelligent, mischievous and, whisper it, also quite the iconoclast himself.

At the end of Phil's rather unenjoyable working period acquiring the Abbey habit he had a brief pint with Denis, and asked him, in something akin to an exasperated tone, 'Why, Denis? Why? Oh why? Please tell me – why does every single person in this building like you to the point of idolatry?'

Denis turned around and with the most Machiavellian look, etched a rictus, almost insane, but still convincing, grin on to his lower face, and Joker-like, traced his finger around the wide expanse of his utterly disarming smile. And he said nothing. And he kept smiling.

If you want your class to like you, then you must give out the signs that you like them: they will then reflect that liking. Smile at them and they will smile back. Go 'Rah' at them and they will go 'Rah' back.

So, in terms of how we use the muscles in our faces, do attempt to keep yours in a sincere smile as often as you are able, even when you are utterly cross, and particularly when you are being wound up. The smile may not work in terms of behaviour management (though it usually will), but it will let it be known to your charges that you are not phased by behavioural issues.

Varieties of smiles

Professional laugher, the Dalai Lama, notes that there are many different kinds of smile: 'Sarcastic, artificial, or diplomatic. Some smiles don't arouse any satisfaction, and some even engender suspicion or fear.' Technically speaking, he's wrong: there are only two kinds of smile, and while Mr Lama appears confident in stating that only 'an authentic smile ... arouses an authentic feeling of freshness', the interesting thing for a professional is that generally human beings are not good at telling the difference between a real and a fake smile. So if you can't manage a sincere smile all the time, a fake smile will generally have much the same result.

The two kinds of smile are classified as a D smile or a non-D smile, after the French neurologist, Duchenne du Boulogne, who first noted them.

A Duchenne (D) smile is when the orbicularis oculi muscle, which encircles the eye, comes into play, raising the cheeks and giving the smiler crow's feet around the eyes. As most people (about 90% of the population) are unable to contract this muscle voluntarily, as 'it does not obey the will',[6] Duchenne recorded it as being the sign which 'unmasks the false friend'. A non-Duchenne (non-D) smile does not involve the eyes and may reasonably be described as being a 'social smile'.

His discovery was promptly forgotten for in the region of 120 years until such point as Paul Ekman, in 1982, rediscovered Duchenne's work as part of Ekman's own investigation into why people smile when they aren't happy. Ekman reports that, 'When a ten-month-old infant is approached by a stranger, the baby's smile will not involve the muscle around the eyes',[7] but that when the baby sees their mother it will. Babies show D-smiles to their mums and non-D smiles to everyone else. He also notes that happily married couples show D-smiles to each other when they meet; unhappily married couples show non-D smiles.'[8]

Of interest to the teacher here is the fact that it isn't always easy to

---

[6] Ekman, 2004, p. 206.
[7] Ekman, 2004, p. 207.
[8] Ekman, 2004, p. 207.

distinguish between the two types.[9] As Ekman notes, 'Most people miss it.'[10] So while you may feel there is an element of fakery to be continually smiling at your students, when beneath the exterior it is Dante's Inferno in your soul, they may not necessarily receive it as a fake smile. In addition, if a non-D, social smile is broad enough, it will actually push the facial muscles, particularly the cheeks, into a position that really quite accurately approximates the eye contours in a real smile. The message here is that if you are going to fake a smile at a student, in order to receive the mirror of it, then make it as broad as possible. You may think that you are giving out the kind of smile that, in the words of Ian McCulloch, 'would shame a politician',[11] but it is not (necessarily) how it will be received.

Facial expression when in conflict

There is a key point at which the communication that you convey with your face is absolutely vital: when a student has lost their self, or is beginning to lose their self to anger. When anger is escalating the professional response is to understand that angry people do not hear much (if anything), and that the only communication that is going to work is to over-communicate positivity with the face and with the body. (It may be that you have to practise this at home in order to get it right, but it really is as simple as adopting your most encouraging and smiley face and ensuring that your body language is open and that you are not spatially threatening.)

Bear in mind, though, that there are a few exceptions to the rule. You will need to alter your technique when you are dealing with students who have specific learning difficulties. If, for instance, you are working with a child who is autistic or who has Asperger's Syndrome, then a smile is of little use, as a defining part of their condition is that they can't read or interpret facial expressions. A thumbs-up signal works well as an agreed signal that everything is okay. A child with special needs, such as Downs Syndrome, will need to know that you are really, really smiling at them, and that you are making it really, really obvious that everything is really, really okay.

In terms of the cycle of transmission and receipt, an expert at managing behaviour will be aware that reflecting anger back to someone who is angry

---

[9] www.answers.com/topic/smiling-2#ixzz1hH1myWs6
[10] Ekman, 2004, p. 205.
[11] Echo and the Bunnymen, 1981.

will cause that anger to escalate by giving the anger a mirror to feed on. Consequently, if you make the decision to communicate positivity, you must also give the student space to calm down, ignoring their behaviour and then talking to them calmly, positively and clearly about what it is you want them to do. By not giving the anger the stimulus it requires to escalate you are instead allowing it to top off, and from there to dissipate.

Body language in the classroom

The body communicates whether you want it to or not, and so it is massively worthwhile being consciously in charge of what signals it is sending out. If you are not, you can easily find that you are unconsciously transmitting signals that damage your ability to control the class, or that affect the students' trust in your sincerity and confidence.

There are different rules for when you are standing in front of the class declaiming and for when you are supporting, either in a one-on-one basis, or in small groups.

Body language and spatial secrets when in front of the class

Where you stand

When Phil was first asked to sit in the back of other teachers' classrooms with a piece of paper and a clipboard and come up with a summary judgement that would be written down in a file that no one ever hopes will be opened, the headteacher who had asked him to do so told him how easy it was to work with teachers who were struggling: 'You'll probably find they're just standing in the wrong place,' she said. And you know what …?

Where you stand is, in the middle – you stand in the middle – at the front. That way the sight lines are equal; that way you are near your kit (whiteboard, either interactive or classic) and, most of all, that way you are positioned in some kind of locus where the symbolic power of being at the centre of things reverberates entirely in your favour. It is at the front in the middle that you must stand if the class chat has become a little too loud, or worse still, if you have lost order. You will not regain order from the side. You stand at the front in the middle.

That is not to say that you never move from there. Most good teachers will attempt to lend a little white space to the diatribe, so to speak, by not staying in exactly the same place for a full hour of them chatting: they will alter the focus point for their students to keep them on their toes, by moving from one point to another. Be aware, though, there is a right and a wrong way to do this. The wrong way is to wander around aimlessly and indecisively, moving around like a drunken bumblebee. This transmits to our students that we are either drunk, or do not really know what we are doing. The correct way of altering the focus point is picking a point in the room that you are going to move to, shut up, move there, ensure that you still have the focus of the class and then begin delivering again from your new focus point.

How you stand

There is also a right and a wrong way to stand. If you are delivering a lengthy monologue to a class, you should focus on having your head tall as this communicates confidence; your shoulders should be low and relaxed as this communicates your ease in the situation. What you should certainly not do is dance about in front of the class in the manner of a Year 7 student doing their first ever class presentation without a piece of sugar paper to hide behind. You know the thing: where you impersonate the world's most reluctant and least funky dancer, making like an indecisive, 'crab on a solo' dance – side together, side together, side together, side: shuffling from point to point, communicating your utter lack of ease in the situation. This kinaesthetic noise is utterly distracting for the students and it will cause them to drift off into analytical thought about your method of delivery rather than profound contemplation of the material you are delivering.

Open and closed body language

Initially, this seems to be intellectually facile and, certainly, neither notion is difficult to understand. However, these all too easy concepts can be tricky to assimilate on a behavioural level. You will understand them without having to think twice, but being able to fluently incorporate that understanding into your behavioural lexicon can be substantially more difficult. You have to train yourself to maintain open body language at all times and that takes commitment and practice, because in many instances you are asking your body to act against its instinct.

Put broadly, open body language transmits that you are relaxed, enthusiastic and are ready to encompass any new experience. Closed body language communicates the opposite: it signals that you are frightened, closed off and are, potentially, at least, dismissive of any new idea or behaviour.

The manifestations of either are quite obvious, and are easily explained. Someone who is displaying open body language will have it all uncrossed: arms, legs, the lot. Someone with closed body language will be the opposite: everything will be crossed – arms, legs, the lot.

It is reasonable to suppose that this stuff all goes back, as everything tends to do, to matters of the genitals (and to the other vital organs too). In crossing our legs we are protecting what postwar mums would have described as being our 'privates' from assault or attack; in crossing our arms we are protecting our torsos. Closed body language conveys that we believe ourselves under potential threat (whether we do or not – it is how it is received that is important), and, as such, is not communicating our confidence and our openness to our charges. While standing in front of a class it is important therefore that we keep our body language in the realm that communicates our ease with the people we are working with and the situation we are in.

As a thought exercise, please spend a few moments imagining what your body language in the classroom would be if you were to model each of the five c's of compassionate communication (see Chapter 1). What would calm look like? How would you use your body to show that you are confident? Is it possible to be clear in terms of the way your body communicates? How can you appear compassionate?

Body language and spatial secrets when supporting students

Here the spatial significance of your height, or otherwise, comes into play. It is a demonstrably magnificent idea to use your knees for what they were designed for: kneeling. This is covered in more detail in the section 'Do employ the great behavioural management secret' on page 47, but broadly speaking, when you are showing a student that you are an expert (that, so to speak, you are better than them at something), then you should ensure that spatially they are the dominant party in the transaction. If you kneel beside them, you are in no way confrontational, and it eases the transaction as you impart knowledge.

There is also an optimum position and gesture when you are using the technique of questioning students to lead them to the construction of their own thoughts and conclusions. This is to have your head bowed, in an approximation of deference, and your hands, palms visible, out to the sides of your body in a display of openness that indicates that you propose no threat. You are asking your students to take risks and your body language must encourage their security in that risk taking.

Something you should definitely try to avoid is something that OFSTED refers to as 'aimlessly touring'. This is where you have set a piece of work for students to do and rather than actively engage with students helping them with any problems they have with their work, you wander around the room in no particular direction with no particular intent, no doubt smiling like a benign clown. If you are to support students it must be with intent!

Body language in conflict situations

The time in which it is vital for you to be in control of whatever signals your body sends out is when you are in a conflict situation with a student, and you want that conflict to be resolved rather than to escalate. At this point, everything you have learnt about good body language must be followed. This can be very difficult: when thrust into a conflict situation you will most likely go into an instinctive state, displaying things you do not want to transmit. To avoid transmitting those natural but unhelpful body language postures, you must adopt the professional, trained response, but you will have to work on this, as they will only start to come naturally when you have practiced the response a few times.

It is worth attempting to internalize the following techniques as rules for whenever you are in the classroom, and not just for times of conflict. They apply for everyday classroom teaching and using them on a day-to-day basis will make it all the easier to recall them when they are really needed.

Body language *don'ts* when in class or in conflict

- *Don't hold your chin*: This transmits to students that you are reserving judgement. As you are hiding half your face, you are being less than honest and open about your emotional response. It may be that you feel holding your chin is a signal to students that you are concentrating on what they are saying. This may be what you believe you are transmitting; it may not be what is being received.

- *Don't fold your arms*: This closed body language signal suggests that whatever decision needs to be made has already been made, and it will be received by the student as you communicating to them that whatever they are saying to you will have no impact whatsoever. In addition, it can be perceived as a sign of aggression. Don't do it!

- *Don't body hold:* You may not even be aware that you are doing this. Check if you unconsciously wrap one of your arms around yourself, maybe touch your elbow or give yourself a consoling rub, cuddle or pat as you enter a conflict situation. If you do, unlearn the habit: it appears insecure and transmits weakness to your students.

- *Don't indulge in any repetitive body language signals:* These come in an alarmingly wide variety. Chief among them perhaps is the staccato speech accompanied by a pointed finger that you may well remember your mother doing to you: 'And *(point)* – if *(point)* – I've *(point)* – told *(point)* – you *(point)* – once *(point)*   I've *(point)* – told *(point)* – you *(point)* a – *(point)* – thousand *(point)* – times *(point)*.' Needless to say this comes across as rather aggressive and antagonistic. Other repetitive signals include continually patting pockets or tapping the foot. Both of these transmit the wish to be elsewhere; particularly the feet, which are actually indicating their owner's desire to move away from the situation – they are so eager to get away they cannot help telling the student.

- *Don't increase posture or height:* This indicates that you are ready and willing to enter the realm of physical conflict, and you are subconsciously making yourself look bigger to scare off your opponent. This is a ridiculous piece of behaviour for a professionally trained teacher. The correct position in terms of spatial displays of status is entirely the opposite. (For more on this, see 'Do employ the great behaviour management secret' on page 47.)

- *Don't invade personal space:* The key word here is *invasion*. In stepping over a student's imaginary exclusion zone you are actually plunging them into a sensory landscape over which they have no control and which they have not entered under their own volition: they can smell your breath, your cologne and whether or not it has been a particularly hot day. You are also, in invading their space, theoretically blocking their path from leaving the room if they feel that they need to. In addition, you have no idea what your students' previous experience of the physical has been. An invasion of their personal space could be received as the precursor to them being physically assaulted. This is not a signal that is – at all – liable to calm them.

- *Don't eyeball:* This is confrontational and is a warning sign to the person being eyeballed that they are about to be physically assaulted.

- *Don't speak too much:* You'll often feel the volition to say things when in a conflict situation, you know the kind of thing, noises that come out of your mouth that you think have meaning. Often, however, you will find that what you say doesn't actually have a great deal of meaning or significance at that moment. It may be better not to speak to them at all, at least initially. Saying nothing can be a very good strategy in moments of conflict: it allows the students to have their say, and it also allows them to vent their anger, so that by the time you speak, they will be in a more receptive frame of mind. Just don't storm in blaring meaningless words. In a conflict situation the understanding of language isn't particularly nuanced.

Body language *dos* when in class or in conflict

- *Do locate the exit:* It is better if this is behind you. If you are in a situation where it becomes impossible for either you or the young person to continue with the conversation, there is an escape route.

- *Do sit down:* Try and find a way of sitting down, and – this may well sound a little silly – preferably on a chair. In sitting down you are spatially altering your status so that, as you are the one who is symbolically and literally in the lower position, you are not inhabiting the role of the domineering authority figure who is there to be rebelled against. You are just sitting down on a chair, having a chat about stuff. On matters less liberal, it is also useful to have the chair as a barrier if the student seems to be considering kicking out or hitting you.

- *Do employ the great behavioural management secret:* There are moments in teaching when a technique strikes as an epiphany: when the true significance of the 'pens down' rule is grasped; when the realization dawns that the correct time to stop an activity is when the first person has finished it. This technique is of that groundbreaking level of significance and may well be the most important thing you learn from this book. Employ it, and within a brief period of time it will reduce behavioural incidents in the region of 25%. The technique has a name – it is called 'standing side-on'. If you are in a discussion that has been chiefly prompted by an issue of behaviour, then stand in front of the child and you are in full on, face-to-face confrontation mode: two gunslingers ready to duel and draw. Stand side-on and you are just two humans having a perfectly reasonable chat about something.

  This technique is usefully combined with its close cousin, 'kinking the knees'. This, again, takes away from your physical presence, has you marginally less physically imposing height-wise, and subliminally signals that you are two humans who are of the same status spatially. Furthermore, kinking your knees allows you to push away if necessary. Stand flat-footed and you are more vulnerable: the hamstrings are the chief engines of movement and of getting away. Have them ready. You must also manage and control your breathing, so that you stay calm, and so that you are sufficiently relaxed to be able to move quickly if required.

- *Do maintain critical distance:* Critical distance is two arms' length away. You should keep this distance so you are not invading students' personal space, and so that they can't kick you. Should any assault occur, the feet are often the cause for concern. When the police are trained in this area, they are taught how to maintain critical distance by standing opposite each other with their arms outstretched and only touching fingers. They are then asked to try and kick their partner. And they fail.

Figure 3.1 Kicking policemen

- *Do look away*: If eyeballing students transmits a signal they may well receive as meaning they are under attack, then where should your focus point be? The answer is ... away. Don't gaze directly at the young person; look away at some imagined point in the near distance. This way, it is not about you and it is not about them; it is about something external to the personal. At the same time, keep the student within your peripheral vision, so that you remain sensitive to the body language signals they are transmitting.

- *Do face your palms down:* If you instruct a student to 'Calm down', it is quite likely you will achieve nothing. If we recall that in the region of only 7% of how we communicate is achieved through the words we choose to deploy, then the instruction itself is less articulate than the manner in which it is delivered. Saying, 'Be calm' achieves nothing. You will get a far better result by being calm yourself, as the student will mirror your behaviour. In addition, put your hands out, palms downward, facing the floor and either stay still, or, in the technique that Desmond Morris has observed politicians using when they wish to calm an audience, make three moves downwards with your hands.

- *Do be aware of objects*: Objects can be thrown at you. You don't want this. Some objects are sharp. Blunt ones hurt too.

- *Do ask them to follow you*: This is often a very useful technique to employ. There is nothing confrontational about the instruction or request that they follow you: it can even be delivered in a cheeky and conspiratorial manner. What it serves to do, if it is obeyed – and it usually is – is to take the young person away from the immediate scene of the behavioural infraction. As it distracts them, it also creates some metaphorical distance: away from the scene, a student is able to calm down and gain perspective on recent events far more quickly than if they were still mouldering in the original scene, where all the stimuli that contributed to their anger are still naggingly present.

The power of positive touch

Touch in schools is a difficult and controversial area. Many teachers will give you the advice to never, ever, even consider touching a student, whatever the reason. This advice is there to protect you, the teacher, from any false accusation of misunderstanding that may occur if you do so. There will be many people who regard this as a cardinal rule, and you should weigh up the opinions of those people with our opinions in this book, as it is a very serious area. If you get things wrong, you may very well find that you are unable to work ever again, and what is more, you could find yourself on a register of offenders. The 'never touch a child' rule is not unreasonable.

However, do not believe for a moment anyone who tells you that it is illegal to touch a child; this would be impossible and impractical. What should you do when a small child is falling over and you have the ability to catch them? Let them fall? The law on this is stated quite clearly in the Bristol Guide, which details teachers' legal liabilities and responsibilities. It says, 'It is unnecessary and unrealistic to suggest that teachers should touch pupils only in an emergency … it is inevitable … particularly with younger pupils.'[12]

It continues, 'It may be appropriate to do so in order to give reassurance or to comfort a child … this acceptance that teachers may make physical contact with children is accompanied by the rider that it must be *appropriate*.'[13]

Given that it is legal to do so, and the Department of Education states that in some circumstances it is appropriate, it is our belief that, as a rule, 'do not

---

[12] School of Education, 1997, p. 18.
[13] School of Education, 1997, p. 18.

touch a child' sees things too far through the prism of pessimism and fear, and that it misinterprets the word 'touch' as being a euphemism for abuse. Positive touch, within the strictest of guidelines, can be an important and useful way of communicating. Schools are too often environments in which the physical is discounted and in which we ignore our innate tactile nature as mammals. Touch can be used to reassure, to console, to encourage; it can be the thing that starts up a relationship of trust; it can be the pivotal point in a young person's life – an expression that someone cares, when previously it appeared that no one did.

Experience of positive touch is vital to our well-being as animals. Our clumsily thumbed cousins, the monkeys, provide evidence: an American psychologist by the name of Harry Harlow[14] thought it might be an interesting idea to take them away from their mums and to give them mums instead that were made of chicken wire and cloth. But these new mums were of two different types and formed two separate experiments. There was an economy version and a luxury version: the economy was made of bare wire and the luxury mum was covered in a piece of soft cloth.

In Experiment 1 luxury mum didn't come with the luxury of food, while economy mum was rigged with a bottle of milk. Experiment 2 was the other way around: economy mum had no food while luxury mum provided the bottle of milk. In either case, when a scary man or a picture of a lion was brought into the monkey room the monkeys all fled for the welcoming arms of luxury mum, whether or not she was the one providing the food.

The experiments went further. When placed in a new environment along with the luxury mum, the monkeys would cling to her for comfort, before venturing out to explore. When placed in the room without their surrogate they would run from object to object, blind with terror. When the monkeys who had been mothered by the chicken-wire mum were placed in a new environment with her, they also responded with blind fear. Despite the fact that the chicken-wire mum might have fed them, they acted as if they had no mum at all.

Harlow concluded that in certain primates the need for contact comfort is stronger than the need to explore, that a lack of physical contact is psychologically harmful and that feeding is a less important factor in the mother/child bond than contact.

---

[14] Harlow, 1958, p. 673.

Haptic communication (communication through touch) is a key means of interaction for our species, and it is worth being briefly knowledgeable in its use and rules, so that you don't make mistakes in this area. According to Heslin, we touch for one of five reasons:

1 Functional/Professional
2 Social/Polite
3 Friendship/Warmth
4 Love/Intimacy
5 Sexual/Arousal[15]

Clearly, some of these are more appropriate in school than others. Broadly, though, the use of touch in a classroom, while it may have elements of expressing friendship or warmth, is of the functional/professional variety. As such, any use of touch requires awareness of what Yarborough calls 'a blueprint for touch'; Yarborough explains that there are two distinct body areas: one that people are happy for other people to touch; the other for which the person touching must have permission. The first consists of non-vulnerable body parts, and are the hand, the shoulder, the arm and the upper back. All other parts are vulnerable body parts, and are not to be touched in a classroom situation.[16]

Any use of touch in the classroom must be done with an awareness that people will have different tolerances and that there are cultural aspects of these tolerances that you must respect. Broadly, though, an affirmative touch on any of the non-vulnerable body parts, particularly an affirmative clasp of the lower arm or gentle pat on the back, can be an expression of warmth that sends a special message from teacher to student.

The thumbs do the damage

What particular function do the four fingers perform when you are texting your mother that you will be late? They (merely) support. It is the thumb that does all the hard work. (It is there for more than just the space bar.)

About 60 million years ago the thumb 'declared independence from the

---

[15] Heslin, 1974.
[16] Jones and Yarborough, 1985, pp. 19–56.

other fingers' and since then it has made all the difference: the ability to touch the soft pad of the finger to the pad of the thumb has distinguished us even from our cousins, the chimps, whose ability is less than perfect, and makes their tool using less accurate than ours. As a freelance reviewer wrote in the *New York Post*, 'The fishing rod that a chimp strips of leaves and pokes into a termite nest to bring up a snack is as far as he'll ever get toward orbiting the planets.'

Thumbs are vital; but in terms of contact with students, you will do well to realize that it is the thumbs that do the damage, and that if you have to take someone's arm to lead them away from a situation, there is a correct and a wrong way of holding them.

Try the following experiment to judge the impact of using thumbs. Use your right hand to hold the lower part of your left arm in two different ways. First, place your thumb on the underside of the arm, and your four fingers on the upper side – now squeeze! Hurts doesn't it? Now move the thumb away so that it abuts the fingers and clasp your lower arm as if your hand were a cuff-like Celtic bracelet. This should feel warm and reassuring, and not at all hurtful. It is the thumbs that do the damage. If you are to use the power of positive touch, leave them out of it.

Gesture and culture

Did you know that in Portugal pinching your earlobe between thumb and forefinger means 'It is excellent'? In Italy, however, the same gesture is taken as an imputation that the person being gestured to (or at) is gay. This is further complicated by the fact that, in Spain, the same gesture means, 'You are a sponger – hanging off me like a lobe hangs off an ear.' Imagine a Spanish restaurant in which the waiter asks the Portuguese diner, 'How was your food?' 'Excellent,' replies the diner, gently pinching his earlobe to affirm how much he enjoyed the meal.

Now, obviously no one likes to be thought of as a sponger, and the Spanish waiter's temper is ignited. He runs to the Patron, Giovanni, who asks the waiter to repeat what caused him such offence. The waiter pinches his earlobe, and the Patron looks nonplussed. 'What's so wrong with that?' he asks. 'You are gay.'

Many of the more challenging schools in the country are multicultural, and you will encounter children from many different races and creeds. You must differentiate your behaviour accordingly, particularly in terms of the way you express yourself with gesture, facial expression and body language, taking into account, as exemplified above, that different gestures mean different things in different cultures. Otherwise, you may find yourself in the situation where you are supporting an Iraqi student, who asks you what you think of his work, and you reply with – what you think – is the universal hand gesture of 'A – okay', blithely unaware that the student has received this communication as it is generally received in his country, as the universal sign for 'bum-hole'. Each culture has its own version of the silent language of the body. Of particular note are the following important variances:

- Do not ever touch a child who is a different gender to you if they are Islamic or Jewish. You are treading in very sensitive waters culturally, and will cause enormous offence. Equally, those in many Asian cultures do not touch strangers, so avoid greetings with a handshake.

- Islamic and Hindu people regard the left hand as dirty – as it is for matters of the toilet – touching with that hand may be received as insulting.

- Avoid the palms upward 'come here' gesture, as Korean, Filipino and Latin people find this offensive.

- Many people from South-East Asian cultures use the smile as a mean of hiding emotion, as expressions of emotion are regarded as unseemly. You will therefore have difficulty in reading how they are feeling, and will need to use language to find out.

- Be aware of the immense cultural differences in terms of the significance of eye contact. In Afro-Caribbean culture and in many of the South-East Asian cultures lack of eye contact is taken as a sign of deference and respect for authority. Do not superimpose Western ideas of lack of eye contact being a sign of insolence, or lack of engagement. However, remember also that Arabic cultures regard prolonged eye contact as important, and people who do not reciprocate as being untrustworthy.

- You may perceive slouching as rude; most Northern European nations do. Your student, who is not from Northern Europe, may not understand your anger at this, so don't express it.

- Turkish people find hands in pockets and crossed legs to be outrageously rude.

Your voice

As a professional reciter of educational stuff you will be aware that the voice is a massively important part of the teacher's armoury. It is useful to focus on how to employ this as a tool as persuasively as possible.

Voice production

You will find that a 30- or 40-year career in teaching will take an excessive toll on the various parts of you that produce your voice; therefore for your voice to survive long term you have to learn to look after it. This means no shouting: apart from it being a bad behaviour management technique, it's really, really bad for your voice, and it also means that you have to learn a few basic amateur-dramatic fundamentals about voice production. If you strain your throat, you'll find teaching a difficult class absurdly hard, as you will be squeaking and barking while they dismantle the furniture.

The engine room of the voice is the diaphragm: this is a muscle at the bottom of the stomach that forces the air out of the lungs, and it is mastery of this as a means of creating an impressive noise that will save you from losing your voice. If you want to make a big noise, then you must inhale to the bottom of your stomach and then use the diaphragm to force the air out. It is in having enough breath for decent voice production that we avoid pushing the voice out from the throat, which is the root of all sore throats.

You would do worse than to learn a few of the techniques that dramatic types might employ before doing a workshop, as follows:

Breathe in through the nose to the count of three then out through the mouth to the same count. Do this a few times before bringing the count up to five, then to seven and finally to ten (which is difficult, if you enjoy to smoke a cigarette). The point here is to be in control of the amount of breath you exhale. This gives you control of the amount of air you need to produce the desired volume without having to go into the dark realms of the shout.

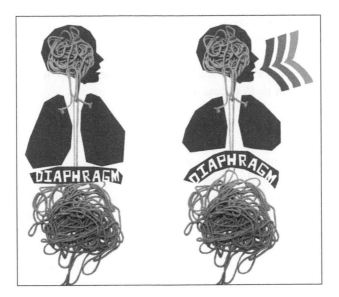

Figure 3.2 Diaphragm

Decent, rehearsed diaphragm control is a prerequisite for a voice that lasts the course of a term.

The breath that you produce with that particular muscle resonates in your head and the sound is then produced through the mouth with the teeth, tongue and lips all having their part to play. (Are you keeping up at the back?) The reason we have stated this oh-so-obvious fact is that it is your use of these facial tools – the teeth, tongue and lips – that allows you to enunciate. Many is the poor child in a school of whatever stripe who has to suffer their teacher's over-accented, poorly enunciated speech. We have seen lessons delivered in such a style that they were completely unintelligible to the students who were sitting there dumbly wishing they could make out a word that their teacher said.

If you recall that one of the five keys of decent communication is clarity, then it is, erm, clear that you must be intelligible when you speak. If enunciation is an issue for you, and be honest with yourself – if anyone has ever mentioned it, it is – then take the time and effort to sort it out. A favourite exercise of ours, as it is amusing enough not to be completely irritating, is to pick two consonants at random and then intone the *William Tell Overture*, switching from one consonant to another within each line:

Bu-bu-bu-bu-bu-bu-bu
Der-der-der-der-der-der

And so on. Practice a little at this and it will get your mouth in all the right kind of shapes for perfect enunciation.

Vocal tone

If we cast our minds back to Mehrabian: what we are after is making automatic our ability to convey the fact that we like the people we are working with and, from then, to have that liking mirrored back to us. Remember, Mehrabian's formula has 38% of conveying liking being expressed through 'vocal liking'. So your aim must be to arrive at a place where you can instantaneously manifest the tone that conveys to your students that you delight in their individual and corporate company.

In the same way as body language can be manipulated for different situations in the school, so can your tone of voice. There should be a difference between your front of class voice, the voice employed while supporting a student (which should be *sotto voce*) and the voice you use in conflict situations.

The front of class voice

Once you have mastered how to pump up the volume using your diaphragm, then – broadly speaking – Bob's your lobster. However, there are other unsubtle vocal tricks that can be used to maintain the interest of an uninterested group of young people, not the least of which is employing dynamic range.

If you recall the American cartoon *Charlie Brown*, his experience of his teacher talking was a soporific sludge of 'mwah-mwah-mwah' sounds which delivered no meaning at all. It was just an adult going on about stuff. We do not mean to sit in judgement of Charlie Brown's teacher's ability to plan an inspiring lesson, but her delivery clearly left something to be desired.

Sitting as a student listening to someone older than you talk about something you aren't particularly interested in is perhaps an unappealing enough concept to make you empathize with your students' perception of their plight as being purgatorial, but when it is combined with delivery that is as dull as a cloudy Tuesday afternoon in early February, then something has to change.

A means of retaining the attention of a class while delivering the teacher-she-speaks part of a lesson is to be aware of, and to utilize, the concept of dynamic range. This is when you use differing levels of volume so that you are not at constant monotone level while you deliver your lengthy monologue. If you think back to a teacher going on for a long time when you were a school student it will have been the sheer monotony of their tone that had you crawling the walls in agonized boredom.

It is often assumed that a full tonsorial subshout level should be used when declaiming at the front of a class. Actually, the opposite approach pays far more dividends. Put yourself in the situation that you are in a room with someone who speaks at 'has headphones in and is listening to really loud rock music' volume. Is their display of volume more likely to make you incline towards them or shrink away? The latter, clearly. So it is in a classroom; rather than bluster in making everyone feel frightened, uncomfortable and claustrophobic, you should lower your voice: this will make your students more interested in what you are saying, will have them incline towards you; its implied intimacy will have them more interested in what you have to say. It will also make them take their fingers out of their ears.

Another useful trick in terms of how you use your voice is to employ a pause quite regularly. This lets your students process what you have been saying and allows a little white space in the diatribe. The truly expert teacher will be masterful with a pause, and will be able to hold their audience's attention without saying anything at all, or even moving, for a greater period of time than anyone would think possible. The deliberate pause for effect is something you can experiment with – and have fun with – till it eventually becomes a really useful classroom control device.

Your voice when in conflict

A conflict situation requires that you 'drop a tone'. You need to transmit calm through your voice, and you do this by deliberately pitching your voice a tone down from where it might normally be: both tonally and in terms of the volume you pitch it at. Your voice should be modulated to convey control and you should consciously speak significantly slower than you would in any other situation.

Language in the challenging school

While the language we choose in the classroom may not be of as much importance as the way we say it, nor anywhere near as significant as to whether we are smiling or not, it remains an area in which we can choose to do the right thing or can inadvertently head off in entirely the wrong direction.

You had – or still have – parent(s). You have been a child, and you will probably still recall some of the ways in which your parent(s), teachers or other significant adults talked to you that you found intolerable, so start by trying to avoid these. Also, there is a rich array of linguistic tics that you should studiously avoid. You may find that they are your natural response to a given situation, but they will not help you to manage behaviour as effectively as you would like. In fact, it is entirely appropriate to view such phrases as word 'traps', as they can be construed as being disempowering and as conveying aggression and, therefore, may inadvertently trigger further displays of the behaviour you are attempting to stop.

Language *don'ts*

Avoid the following phrases

- *It's not as bad as all that.* How do you know? It might be. You are not inside their head.

- *Grow up.* This is an utterly illogical instruction: a child will not grow at an accelerated rate simply because you have instructed them to do so. Furthermore, it is not possible for a child to be older than their brain, and it is the developmental stage that their brain is at that is, more likely than not, causing them to behave in the manner for which you are now upbraiding them. It is infuriating and humiliating to be told to grow up; infuriating a child is not going to lead to seamless behaviour management, and humiliating them is likely to land you in a whole heap of trouble.

- *Can't. Mustn't. Shouldn't. Couldn't.* This is overly emphatic language and, to reverse a Bing Crosby lyric, 'accentuates the negative'.

- *Yeh, but. No, but. Yes. No. Yes. No.* Everyone recognizes the figure of Vicky Pollard. She is a satire of young ladies of a particular subset of a certain social class, and was not intended as a role model for teachers. Besides, you are meant to be modelling the use of appropriate Standard English.

- *Don't be silly. Don't be stupid.* Here you are diminishing students' concerns, making them appear small and irrelevant. They will not feel that they are being silly or stupid, and in using this language you are explicitly stating that you think they are.

- *With respect.* This, of course, means that you are about to be disrespectful.

- *You kids. You lot!* This is best left for the end line of a *Scooby Doo* cartoon ('I would have got away with it if it wasn't for you meddlin' kids!'). This groups together an array of individuals, who have individual souls and individual responses, into a homogenous lump of objectified, non-human matter. Indeed, any form of depersonalized language should be avoided. In making the young people whose development we are in charge of into objects, or even syndromes or conditions, we are subconsciously denying them their rights as humans.

Avoid the following types of language

- *Degrading language:* Obviously, language that seeks in any way to degrade is not the linguistic choice that should be employed by anyone with a teaching certificate: it reduces a child's sense of their own worth.

- *Overemoted language or referring to your own emotional life:* This is an amateur's trick and is, moreover, a form of passive aggression. Introducing your own feelings, then trying to make the other person responsible for those feelings is actually one of the behaviours from children that you will sometimes have to be responsible for managing. Remember, you are meant to be the adult in the interaction. Remember, as well, that as the adult, you are not to indulge in bouts of transference, in which you transfer the anger that you have been caused by another person or another situation, and transpose it on to the current situation. Yes, your wife/husband may have left you and your dog may have just died, but this should not be relevant when you are a professional responsible for the life chances of children.

- *Threatening language:* Avoid any threats of any kind. If you have to take retributive action, or carry out a consequence, do so, and do so calmly. Do not, at any point, make a desperate attempt to steal back the power you have given away in an exchange by threatening a consequence and informing the child that they will regret their actions because of that consequence. You will come across like a five-year-old: 'I am taking my ball back. And then you will be sorry.' Erm, grow up.

- *Repetitive language:* Be aware, too, that repetitive language, language in which you repeat yourself, where you say the same thing over and over again in different ways, in which you merely repeat words you have already said ... can often be a trigger for an outburst of challenging behaviour.

Language *dos*

Having just read what language to avoid, you can use these as a broad brush to examine the varieties of language you should employ in a challenging class. If you should avoid saying, 'It's not as bad as all that', then the obverse is that you should always attempt to be empathetic in your choice of words, for example: 'I know how you feel' or 'I can see you're upset.'

Indeed, in a conflict situation you can sometimes successfully diffuse an incident by verbalizing what you think the individual is trying to communicate through their behaviour. This lets the student know that you are taking them seriously, and helps the student recognize their own emotional state. As Daniel Goleman says, if you can put a name to an emotion, it is yours. You own it.[17] Simply informing a student that they are angry, or that you recognize their anger, can be a very successful diffusion technique. As an illustration of how well this can work, here is an account of a situation that occurred in which both the authors played a part.

---

[17] Goleman, 1995.

The more temperamental of the two of us, (Phil) was incensed by the actions of a colleague and was spitting at walls! As a result, Phil would have walked out of the building and got directly on to the first bus home without passing go, had not a small part of his brain informed him that it was a better idea to storm into John's office and kick over a few chairs.

Phil: (Storms into office – resists temptation to kick over any chairs only because there aren't any) Arrrrrrrrgh!

John: (Pause) *(Note here that he says nothing at all.)*

Phil: Argh! I told you that I am only happy to work here when I am treated with a little professional respect!

John: (Pause) *(And continues to say nothing.)*

Phil: And I am being treated like a complete idiot!

John: (Pause) *(More nothing.)*

Phil: I said, I am not being treated with professional respect at all!

John: I can see that you are angry. *(Here John is aware that were he to reflect the anger it would have given it a mirror with which to escalate. The key is not to do anything that will make it increase: 'If I'm calm you can't get any more angry.' In reflecting calmness back to a display of anger he ensured that the anger topped off and would start to diminish. He also wanted Phil to reflect on how he was behaving himself rather than sitting in judgement on it. The key in exchanges such as these is to 'drop a tone', make your voice softer and lower than it might otherwise have been.)*

Phil: Did you hear me?[18]

John: Yes. I am listening. *(John felt that Phil's chief concern in the school was that he was not being listened to, and, as such, was feeling powerless. In echoing his concern in a literal manner he acknowledged that the chief issue did indeed exist, and that he would not commit the same act.)*

Phil: What do you think?

John: I think it's not about you.

Phil: Yes it is … it feels like it is.

John: You are not the most important person in this.

---

[18] You will note that the exclamation marks disappear altogether after, 'I can see that you are angry.'

Phil: I am to me.

John: What are we here for?

Phil: What?

John: What are we here for?

Phil: To get paid, of course. (You ridiculous, moral hypocrite.)

John: And in order to get paid whose interests are we here to serve?

Phil: The kids, of course. Stop treating me like an idiot.

John: So, it's not about you, is it?

Phil: (grudgingly) No. It's not.

John: Which path of action would further the kids' achievement? (*This question is intended to get the person displaying the anger to come up with a solution himself.)*

Phil: Mine, of course.

John: So, we do what you are suggesting. But we do it for the right reason: because it is the best path for the kids. It's not about you.

Phil: Thank you for patronizing me. It made me feel very small.

John: That's okay. It was a professional obligation. You were behaving like a baby.

In this example you can see John applying many of the techniques that we've suggested for use in conflict situations. First, he says nothing at all, giving the anger nothing to reflect against, nothing to use as purchase with which to escalate. He then expresses understanding of the fact that Phil is angry, and chooses the modality with which he expresses this: he says, 'I can see' as opposed to 'hear' or 'feel'. He then alters that modality to match Phil and expresses Phil's concern back to him. He then asks a series of questions leading Phil to choose the correct path of action for himself. He is in no way confrontational, nor is he didactic. He allows the madman to achieve a sane response himself.

Challenge, Understand, Define, Search, Agree

In the above scenario John used what behavioural experts call the CUDSA technique. When you are in a situation in which anger between two students has boiled over and they are in a potentially dangerous situation, then there is a simple path to follow that will often diffuse that anger: *Challenge, Understand, Define, Search, Agree.*

The searching for their own solution – they must find it

Use of this technique will entirely diffuse an escalating situation. Simply asking a series of questions, in the correct order, can result in the student transforming from a boiling vial of molten lead into something entirely calmer and more biddable.

When you have a conflict in class that you think is likely to erupt into an imminent display of violence (or, indeed, has just escalated into the early stages), and you have managed to isolate one of the combatants, your first query must be, 'What's up? What's wrong?' And crucially, 'How can I help?' This query is the *challenge* stage and is predominantly there to engage the combatant in a discussion.

In the discussion you are able to move to the next stage, which is for you, the teacher, to display *understanding* of the issues they are facing.

The next question is to ask the combatant what the root of the issue is, and can be as baldly expressed as that: 'Tell me what the issue/problem is?' This will be greeted by a response, which you then define. The *define* stage is where you just repeat back what has been said to you, without imposing any consequence.

You then ask how it can be sorted out (*search*) and come to an agreement over the chosen path of action (*agree*).

The CUDSA technique in action

Teacher: What's wrong? How can I help?*(challenge and understand)*
Student: He called my mother a prostitute.
Teacher: You are telling me that he called your mother a prostitute. Is that right? *(define)*
Student: Yes.
Teacher: What would you like me to do? *(search)*
Student: Tell him she doesn't do that any more. She's got a much better job down Tesco's.
Teacher: Okay. So we are agreed that I am going to tell him that your mother is not a prostitute and that she now works on the checkout at Tesco's. Is that right? *(Agree)*
Student: Yes.

Job done. World saved. Basically, you've done nothing and it's all resolved.

Using positive language

Go back to the list of phrases that one should avoid, and turn them around; if one is to avoid 'can't', 'mustn't', 'shan't' and 'couldn't' as their negativity are disempowering, then it follows that using positive language, for example 'you can' and 'you could', puts the student in charge of both their own actions and of the consequences that will come from those actions. If it is feeling disempowered that leads a student to be angry, then use of this positive language removes that particular trigger for that anger. In the same way, if we are not to say, 'Don't be silly' or 'Don't be stupid' as these are implied labels, then, again, if we reverse it, it is clear that one thing we should be telling our students is that they are clever.

It can be shocking when working in a challenging school to discover the degree to which students regard themselves as being unintelligent. This limiting form of self-protection has come about because it is a message they have received from somewhere else, either the home environment or from the school system. It is your job to reverse that message. Find out what the young person is good at and you tell them about it! Everyone has a part of themselves that they suspect exists, and further suspect is really special, but it takes a great teacher to be able to locate this part of the person and to tell them about it.

Your use of praise, in time, will be a substantive reason that you win over a difficult student or whole class. Sincerely telling a student that you think a certain aspect of their work, or a certain aspect of their personality, is 'brilliant' makes it very difficult for them to dislike you. In praising, descriptively, you are giving reward for good work or behaviour, and are therefore keeping it on the agenda. This naturally reinforces your expectations of the social norms you want in the class.

It is worth being proactive with this: do not only use praise when in crisis situations, 'You did so well last week.' Use it liberally, so that you create within your classroom, a praise culture. Catch them *doing good*, as it were, and they will be less likely to be caught doing badly.

Differentiate your language

In managing behaviour, you should do it individually. You cannot hold a whole class to account when only half of them are up to no good.

When dealing with young people you must obey the cardinal rule: challenge the behaviour and not the person. 'This particular piece of behaviour is unacceptable' is a massively different message to, 'You are unacceptable.' Likewise, 'When you talk over me it stops the rest of the class from learning' communicates very differently from, 'You are stopping the rest of the class from learning.' By singling out in your language the piece of behaviour you want altered, you are not being accusatory about the person. If you make a distinction in the choice of words you use between what you think about the child and what you think about the action, you will have better results, as it is more likely that a person will recognize the need to change a piece of behaviour than their whole personality.

Ultimately ...

As is the case with body language, your choices in terms of the words that you use should be affected by the five c's of compassionate communication (see page 9). The language you employ should be *calming*; you should attempt to be *confident* in its use; *clear* in your instructions, and your stated expectations should be *compassionate* and *consistent*.

Reward systems

Reward systems can be a cause for controversy among staff, particularly for those who think that an education is a reward in itself, and that external forms of motivation merely trivialize this key message. There is the further issue that, after Key Stage 3, many kids begin to view the culture of the certificate and public clapping as being both childish and more than a little embarrassing. However, this accepted, there is a logical reason behind such systems, and it is worth spelling out how they work.

They operate as positive reinforcement of good behaviour, and supplement formal behaviour management procedures by keeping positive attitudes to learning on the agenda, prompting repeated good behaviour. When these systems (such as the vivo miles system) dispense with the smiley face and gold sticker approach to pupil rewards, and put cinema tickets, bikes and fishing trips on the agenda, the take-up with students in the later years of their education can be substantial.

Dress code

We'll get this one covered here, as how you dress is very much part of the message you give your students about whether you mean business or not.

In the 'olden days', the best advice regarding what you wear to work was to observe how everyone else was dressed and attire yourself accordingly. Today, many schools have a written dress code for teachers, which will generally stipulate that you should dress smartly: a suit and tie and shoes for the male and, erm, whatever they want to wear for the ladies. The absurd sexism of these rules, or the utter stupidity of thinking that wearing a piece of string the shape of a noose round the neck is in some ways a sign of professionalism, has in no way ever caused the straights to doubt themselves, and so men are required to be suited, booted and packaged like trussed-up penguins and women can wear anything they like that doesn't reveal too much décolletage, or into which they have not had to be poured.

There is a borderline rationale behind smart attire for teachers. And that is … that the kids prefer it. Kids like their teachers to dress smartly.

Whatever your own politics on being told what you are allowed to wear or not, there are a few principles that, if your school gives you sufficient respect as an adult to allow you to choose what you wear, you should bear in mind:

- Don't wear jeans. Or trainers.

- Ladies – be discreet with the make-up, the jewellery and anything that will have hormonal boys focusing on parts of your body, when they should be focusing on the wisdom of your words. Low-cut tops or very short skirts will not actually make you into an object, but they will make 'what you look like' send a far bigger message than you want sent.

Test yourself

	Very confident	Confident	Not confident	Huh?
Are you who you should be externally?				
I am aware of Mehrabian's ideas of 'liking'.				
I can convey 'liking' with my facial expressions.				
I know the difference between D smiles and non-D smiles.				
I know how to manage my facial expression when in conflict.				
I know where and how to stand when in front of a class.				
I know how to use my body when supporting a student.				
I know the difference between 'open' and 'closed' body language.				
I know the body language don'ts to avoid when in conflict.				
I know the body language do's when in conflict.				

I use positive touch.				
I am aware that, when physically intervening, thumbs do the damage.				
I am aware of cultural differences in gesture.				
I can use dynamic range.				
I drop my tone of voice in conflict situations.				
I know what language to avoid.				
I know what language to use.				
I present myself professionally.				

Chapter 4
Do you understand your students' behaviour?

Things we think we can't change

The belief that things cannot be changed is a significant barrier to happiness. If you feel that you can't change something, that you are stuck in an unhelpful pattern of behaviour which keeps repeating itself with minor modifications as it pours ever onward into a downward spiral, then, both in the classroom and in life, you are likely to find happiness at worst entirely elusive, at best significantly tarnished. But there are things we cannot change. These, arguably, we have to accept.

Or should we? Is it possible to change the unchangeable?

Take a second away from the book, please. Grab a pen and paper and write down five things in your own life that you believe you are not able to exert any influence over: things that you cannot change. Be as brutally honest with yourself as you are able: if it is your dad's temper say so; if it is a particular teacher's treatment of you when you were a child, then record this too.

The role of optimism in our thinking

The brain is organized in a way that enables optimistic beliefs to change the way that we view and interact with the world around us, making optimism a self-fulfilling prophesy. Without optimism, the first space shuttle might never have been launched, peace in the Middle East would never have been attempted, rates of remarriage would likely be

non-existent, and our ancestors might never have ventured far from
their tribes and we might all be cave dwellers still, huddled together and
dreaming of light and heat.[1]

In his book *Emotional Intelligence*,[2] Daniel Goleman tells a stunning story
about how optimism works, and how perhaps what we think of as optimism
isn't an entirely accurate picture of it. Prior to the 1972 Olympics the coaches
of the American swimming team tried a disastrous experiment: in training,
when timing the practice swims of the team, they told the swimmers that
their time was a fraction of a second slower than they had actually achieved.
The American swimmers had bust several guts in training, believing they
were achieving something near, or ahead of, their personal best, only to
be told that their time was substantially slower than they thought. You can
imagine how frustrating this was, and you can probably put yourself in their
Speedos, and understand why when after 50 swims they had achieved far
less than they thought they had, they just gave up in a strop and took an early
shower. The Americans did not do that well in the pool in Munich, 1972.

Apart from the one swimmer, who was an optimist, and did what
optimists do: he blamed himself! Whenever he achieved a slower time in
training than he felt he had achieved, rather than giving up, he thought that
it must be something he was doing wrong, and that he could improve. He
made changes. Eventually, he won seven gold medals in one Olympics, each
of which was in a new world record time. His name? Mark Spitz.

What this story reveals is that the clichéd and uncomplicated view
of an optimist as someone who always looks on the bright side of life –
the cheery fatalist, if you will – is actually untrue. The real optimist is
profoundly more self-critical and blames themself if something is going
wrong, rather than believing it is a result of external influences that they
cannot change. The real optimist knows that only they can bring about
the necessary changes; the real optimist believes it can be done and takes
action to make it so!

Your mindset with a difficult class (or school) is key. As in all other
aspects of life, you are only a failure if you start blaming someone other than
yourself. An optimistic approach to the difficult class is to go in equipped

---

[1] Sharot, 2012, pp. xvi–xvii.
[2] Goleman, 1995.

with the rueful understanding that, if you are not in control of the class's behaviour, then it can be nobody's fault but your own, and that, to paraphrase stand-up educationalists Dave Keeling and David Hodgson, if you are the problem then you are also the solution.[3] You will not help yourself by blaming the young people you are teaching for being what they are: they cannot help this. It is your job to manage their behaviour, and if you are not managing to do this, then, like Mark Spitz, you must make changes.

That is not to say that in behaving in what is clearly an unacceptable manner in a class is to be forgiven, or laid at the feet of circumstance – 'They can't help it, they've had a difficult time.' They can help it, but they need a firm leader who is prepared to apply a range of strategies to get on top of things, and who is prepared, if necessary, to change their view of that behaviour – to understand it.

Look again at your list of things you think you can't change. What actions or behaviours could you take to make them better? Go back to what you have written and think.

Many of the points in our life that we regard as fixed are not necessarily so, certainly in terms of how we relate to them. No, we cannot change the past, but we can change our attitude to it. No, we cannot change our parents, but we can change the way we relate to them. No, we cannot change our own education, but we can change someone else's; we can change the education of thousands; we may even be able to change the nature of education itself.

But it is not enough to be in control of our own attitudes and behaviour. This is only a starting point. To be able to control the behaviour of a class in a challenging school you must have some understanding of the root causes of that behaviour, and that much of what you will be in receipt of is merely generic: a set of animal responses that are entirely natural, and entirely understandable.

In a challenging school you will witness and have to manage episodes of reactive anger on a daily basis. It generally plays out in much the same way for each occurrence, and will certainly follow the same template. Here we move on to examining how reactive anger works, and what you can do to manage it.

---

[3] Keeling and Hodgson, 2011, p. 14.

A look at reactive anger and aggression

Everyone becomes (or is made) angry from time to time, and anger is, by nature, individual: the way we express and manage it is entirely personalized. Anger will generally cause the person expressing it to behave in an irrational manner, and they *may* also respond irrationally.

In the truly challenging class you will see, and indeed be the object of a lot of this emotion: however, you may not realize that what you are witnessing has a name and that you personally will (generally) not be the cause of it. It goes by the name of aggression, a manifestation of anger, and generally it will be the situation that has caused it, not you! (Though, y'know: there's a fair to middling chance that you did cause it.)

Some of the forms through which anger (and aggression) are expressed are not obvious, and initially you will not recognize them as being manifestations of a pathological condition.

Let's start with a brief look at why you may see quite so much of it.

First, anger can be appallingly seductive, as it makes us feel powerful. It is normal and it is natural. It is ubiquitous – even God is prone to the odd outbreak of wrath – and there is always a reason for it (though, to paraphrase Benjamin Franklin, 'Just never a good one.')[4]

Anger will be perceived by some of the young people with whom you work as an attribute or an ability. And indeed it is. It is not only used as a reaction to a dangerous situation, but also as a bargaining technique, and can be consciously feigned quite successfully in order to manipulate others.

As a footnote, we, as humans, are inclined to attribute higher social status to someone who is displaying anger than we are to someone who is displaying sadness. We perceive the angry person as being somehow powerful, and, as such, if we are negotiating with someone and their opening gambit has been to express anger then we are more likely to be flexible in those negotiations. Expressing anger makes us more powerful in any personal exchange, and so it is used, as a technique, quite regularly and often intentionally.

Predominantly, anger is an innate and instinctive chemical response that has evolved to enhance our chances of survival when under threat. But, you

---

[4] Goleman, 1995, p. 59.

might reasonably argue, no one is under imminent threat of being savaged by a prowling lion while safely ensconced in a school full of caring professionals. Why is this instinct so prevalent in an environment in which it is so patently inappropriate?

There are three stages that you need to look out for in managing anger.

The trigger stage

Reactive anger requires an initial trigger. And like a preschool child searching for the geek in the striped sweatshirt in *Where's Wally?* your job is to locate that trigger.

In students, the trigger will often be the result of having been put into a position in which they have been made powerless, or, at least, made to feel so. It is possible that the anger has multiple causes, but the person transmitting it is only cognitively aware of a single one. For a person to express anger they will most likely have a sense that someone, in particular, is responsible, and that that person's actions were both preventable and unnecessary. Frustration on the part of the student could also be a trigger.

Sometimes, though, anger might be a deliberate behaviour, in which the student has worked out that the circumstances are such that it will meet a reward: the teacher will back down, they will be allowed to continue chewing gum, they will gain status in front of their mates. It may also be a socialized response: the pressures of conformity dictate that to avoid losing face the student has to display anger. Alternatively, it may just be a habitual response, or the student may be under the influence of medication. The environment itself may play a part; or it may be a response to, or characteristic of, particular syndromes and disorders, for example Attention Deficit Hyperactivity Disorder (ADHD), or learning difficulties of whatever stripe.

In terms of transference, (where the anger is a response to something that has happened previously and elsewhere, but is being expressed in the here and now), the more serious triggers may include anything that reminds them of previous experiences of abuse, or touches on their unresolved feelings of separation and of loss. Related to this, the potential triggers may be in response to unmet needs, perceived or real. According to Maslow's hierarchy, all humans have a series of needs: basic (food, shelter and heat); safety needs (security, a healthy body); the need to feel loved and to have a sense of belonging; for our self-esteem to be protected, and the need for self-realization. Everyone in the school (staff and students) will be somewhere on the continuum from having none of these met to sitting smugly in possession of a full set of cards. But the absence of any of these needs is likely to lead to expressions of anger.

It could be argued that we are all buzzing along, all of the time, in a permanent state of subdued anger and that it just takes someone to accidentally or deliberately locate and push one of our buttons (the triggers) to move us from a normal state of arousal to what might be termed as an enhanced state. It may be that the trigger is not caused by a person but by a negative reaction to an environment, or it could be triggered by the student knowing that if he displays anger he will be rewarded. All these triggers will move a student to the next stage of escalation: the build-up.

So, what do you as professionals, if you have noted that one of your students appears to have had their anger triggered and appears to be in a state of increasing arousal, do during the triggering stage?

First, you observe, hoping to locate the trigger. It may be that you inform the student that you recognize that they are becoming angry; it may be that you remove the trigger, as this will take away the reason for the student to be angry. At this stage you must make a professional decision as to whether to intervene or not: it may be that the situation will resolve itself without any action on your part.

The build-up stage

The build-up is where the level of arousal has increased and the student's behaviour has become noticeable. At this point you have to make decisions about what sort of intervention and de-escalation techniques will resolve the issue. There are two possible paths from which to choose: *redirection* or *containment*.

Redirection is a fairly unsophisticated distraction technique, but works stupendously well if carried out with the requisite speed: it must be conducted in the space of a millisecond to work properly. First, you briefly employ the gentlest and briskest touch on the lower arm (avoiding any use of the thumb), then with the other hand point a finger at the work the student should be doing. You then say in an upbeat manner something like, 'Yeh, but what about the work?' You may decide to add, 'You did a fantastic piece last week. How's this going?'

Another redirection technique is to use humour. You tactically ignore the cause of the incident and make no reference to it. Instead you say something funny, perhaps self-deprecating, which is totally off-piste, for example: 'My hair looks stupid today, doesn't it?' 'Do you know, my mum still tells me what I am allowed to wear?' 'How many fish can you name?' This can be a relatively high-risk technique as your deliberate use of a non sequitur may go completely over the student's head, and it is likely that they will see you as being mad. However, if they are thinking, 'This teacher is clinically insane', then it is likely that they are no longer brooding on the trigger and you have 'defused' the situation.

Containment is when you recognize a situation is likely to explode and you look to protect the safety of everyone in the room, including that of the student who is currently in a state of arousal. At this stage it can be perfectly appropriate to have the rest of the class leave the room, leaving the individual experiencing the episode to be left alone so that their behaviour can play out without it impinging on the safety of everyone else. There are futher de-escalation techniques you can use at this stage, and these are covered in Chapter 6.

The crisis stage

Here arousal has hit its peak and this can be dangerous territory. The student has, perhaps involuntarily, given in to a hormonal surge that has provided them with sufficient energy for one decisive course of action. The behaviour is displayed and may be manifested through a prolonged disruption in the class, or even worse, an episode of violence and/or destruction.

There are a series of non-verbal signals that will alert you to the fact that physical conflict may occur imminently, and it is worth internalizing them, as it could stop you, or someone else, from being hit. If you note any of the following body language 'tells', then the student is subconsciously showing you signs that they are in a heightened state, and that you are entering the realms of potential violence.

This is animal behaviour. They are in such an enlivened state that their mammalian instincts are taking over, and the physiological changes that you are witnessing have been evolved in order to protect their body from the impending possibility of being mortally hurt. It may be that the threat here is just a classroom disagreement about name calling, but the subconscious doesn't know this, and will react when triggered in such a way as to protect the organism from impending threat.

Any of the following are signals that physical conflict may occur:

- *Direct prolonged eye contact:* This is a direct challenge and an assertion of control and intent. In our experience, angry young people who are about to launch into a physical attack will stare directly at what (or, more specifically, at the particular area) that they are going to attack.

- *Fists clenching and unclenching:* This is preparation for their imminent use. You will probably find at this point that the hands are generally held slightly above the waist, again, in preparation, and the shoulders will tense, ready to throw weight behind the issue.

- *The facial colour at this stage is paler:* There will have been an initial surge of blood to the head to equip the brain with the ammo to make the correct decision, but when the brain is no longer engaged, and the self-preservation instinct has taken over, then the blood rushes away from the head, and into the hands. Consequently, the face gets paler.

These are the signs that an attack is possible; that you are in the region where de-escalation techniques are urgently required. There is a further stage of signals that mean an attack is going to happen.

These signals indicate that the child is just about to hit something or somebody, and they happen in a sequence:

1   The facial colour darkening as blood rushes to the head. Prior to an attack adrenalin makes the heart beat faster and the breathing rate will accelerate.

2   As a result of the input of adrenalin, the child's behaviour will become inconsistent and unpredictable.

3   The head goes back, predominantly to make themselves appear bigger and to keep the chin out of trouble. At this point they will start to stand tall.

4   The leg muscles will tense and the chest will puff out; again as an animal response to make them appear bigger and taller.

5   When the chin goes down this is a biological – and very definite – signal that they are going to attack. It is the body's way of keeping the vulnerable neck out of trouble.

6 Whatsoever the child is looking directly at will be the thing that they attack. If they are looking at a fixed point on the wall, it is the wall that will get it. If they are staring at your nether regions, the same applies. They will kick or punch what they are looking at.

You must intervene here. This stage is relatively brief (even though its intensity may make it seem to last an age – as your career flashes before you). It may be that at this stage physical intervention is appropriate, and you must make a fairly rapid risk assessment.

Physical intervention – the *dos* and *don'ts*

Clearly, your first responsibility during the crisis stage is to protect. In order to do so you must rapidly make a series of decisions about the level of risk that physical intervention involves. Ask yourself the following questions:

- *Do you know the student?* The situation is likely to play out far less smoothly if you do not. The rules of engagement are likely to be entirely different, if, for instance, you have an existing relationship of trust with the young person than if you do not even know their name. If you do not know them, you must assess that physical intervention is less likely to resolve the situation.

- *How many staff are there?* Are you on your own? Being on your own presents you with a few difficulties in terms of physical intervention. You may be overpowered and there will be no professional witness should anything occur that would place you in a difficult situation professionally. Think twice about physical intervention if you are on your own. Make a professional judgement – you must have the power to negotiate the issue; if you feel you do not have the power, call in support.

- *Are you strong enough?* Judge whether your sex, your age or your size suggest that you are at all likely to be injured if you intervene.

- *What is the worst case scenario?* Often you will find that in a fight the appropriate path is to wrap a protecting arm around the person who appears to be losing and to take them away from the situation.

As they are losing, and you are saving them, they will generally offer little resistance to your help. However, they may continue spitting puce curses in the direction of their fellow combatant as you take them away.

- *What is best for the child?* Acting according to the answer to this is a guiding principle in managing the incident.

Your response must be proportional, and if you are to use force then it must be 'reasonable force'. The question here is what is considered reasonable force? Interestingly, there is no hard and fast legal definition of this concept. The Bristol Guide makes reference to section 550A which was added to the 1996 Education Act, acknowledging that 'Section 550A does not cover every situation where it might be reasonable to use force – for example, to defend oneself from attack or to act in an emergency where there is an immediate risk of injury. Its purpose is rather to make it clear that teachers are entitled to intervene in less extreme situations.'[5] The inference that can be drawn here is that you are absolutely entitled to defend yourself if under attack, or to physically intervene if someone else is likely to be injured. Your response must be 'proportionate' and 'reasonable'.

You are entitled to use reasonable force when the following is likely to occur:

- a criminal offence
- injury to the self or injury to another
- damage to property that will lead to the injury of others
- disrupting 'order and discipline'.

Your legal right to use reasonable force is therefore well established – though it is common in schools for students not to be aware of this fact and to tell you in a display of manipulative aggression that you are not allowed to touch them.

Examples of when you are entitled to use reasonable force are also listed. These are:

- when students are fighting

---

[5] School of Education, 1997, p. 19.

- if they appear to be about to commit a deliberate act of vandalism to property
- if they are at risk of causing damage or injury – here the guide specifically refers to 'rough play'
- if they are running in a corridor or stairwell
- if they refuse to leave a lesson when ordered to do so
- if they are seriously disrupting a lesson
- if their actions in trying to leave an environment are liable to put them at risk.

So you are entitled to use reasonable force to eject a student if they refuse to leave a lesson or if they are being disruptive. However, it is a risky strategy and one we do not recommend. We advise that if a student refuses to leave a lesson get a senior manager to deal with it.

The Guide goes on to suggest what this force might be:

- physically interposing between pupils or blocking a pupil's path
- touching, holding, pushing, pulling or leading a pupil by the arm
- shepherding a pupil away by placing a hand in the centre of the back.'[6]

If you are of a mind to physically intervene it is vital that you carry out the risk assessment first, asking yourself the questions we listed above. There is absolutely no point in going in like Rambo with a student who is twice your size and who is uneven of temper: you will need backup; otherwise you are going to get hurt and your career could be in trouble. You must balance what is best for the child along with what is best for the community. What is best for the community is not that a valuable member of it, a teacher – you – is forcedly humiliated or brutalized in front of an audience of young people, and then has to sit in a disciplinary hearing in which they are accused of inappropriate physical contact. Yes, you must think what is best for the child, but if what is best for the child involves you getting beaten up, then don't do it.

---

[6] School of Education, 1997, p. 20.

The recovery stage

The state of arousal after the incident dissipates following the adrenalin surge; but it does so slowly. The person remains in a state of readiness – a hair trigger state – awaiting a further stimulus that will decide the next action. And this state lasts for a substantial period of time as anger gradually dissipates (in the region of 45 minutes).

At this stage of the incident, you should reassure the young person, and at the same time maintain your management of the incident so that it doesn't flash into action again. We have all been in the situation where we have had an argument, either with a partner, a colleague, or a student, and have attempted to make up or apologize for our contribution to that argument too quickly, only for it all to blow up in our faces again: to have the argument reignite, this time more furious than ever. This is related to anger's reluctance to die down as quickly as we might wish it to. Cognitively, we are able to recognize that perhaps we have been at fault, but the subconscious, hormonal dance that takes place in a dank cave far beneath our powers of cognition has it otherwise. Both parties are still in that state of emotional readiness to rumble, and it only takes the mildest of further negative stimulus to precipitate another full-blown fight!

The student may go through a variety of emotional states during this part of the process, and it may be that the level of arousal returned to is lower than usual and that post-event depression is experienced. The focus here should be on the student returning to normal as quickly as possible, but at the same time you should be taking steps to reduce the likelihood of the incident reoccurring.

And there will be paperwork!

In order to protect yourself from any accusations that might arise of inappropriate behaviour, you must first ensure that a senior manager is informed orally of the incident, then you must write a report. The report will include the following:

- The name(s) of the students involved, and when and where the incident took place.
- The names of any staff or pupils who witnessed the incident.
- The reason that force was necessary.
- How the incident began and progressed, including details of:

- the students' behaviour and what was said by each of the parties
- the steps taken to calm/defuse the situation
- the degree of force used, how it was applied and for how long.

• The students' response and the outcome of the incident.

• Details of any injury suffered by the student(s) and others, and of any damage to property.[7]

Managing your own anger in a professional situation

Think of a recent situation in which you succumbed to the charms of becoming that tempestuous cauldron of boiling metal. What was the result?

What are the differences between how you express anger in a personal situation, such as experiencing a bout of 'road rage', compared with when you are in a professional situation? When you get angry in a professional situation what is the effect of it?

One of us (John) admits that when they are angry in a professional situation they are prone to quietly seething, but crucially this seething will be characterized by 'going calm'. And while this might not be enormously good for your health in the long term, it is certainly a more professional way of conducting yourself than kicking chairs.

As an example of why you should learn how to manage your own anger in a professional situation, remember this tale. The first time that one of the authors realized the full potential impact of his physicality on a student was when he stood up in anger. He was not particularly angry, but felt that it was time to express that anger in a fairly moderate display. He stood in a doorway close to a Year 6 girl. He is quite tall. His sheer presence scared the girl so much that she urinated. It is a brutal experience to be quite so humiliated, and it is a brutal experience to have been the cause of that humiliation. Beware your understandable human anger in a professional situation. It may cause something horrific to happen to a child.

---

[7] School of Education, 1997, p. 20.

Test yourself

	Very confident	Confident	Not confident	Huh?
Do you understand your students' behaviour?				
I understand the pivotal importance of optimism in all situations.				
I know what causes reactive anger.				
I can recognize a trigger and remove it.				
I know the stages of arousal in anger.				
I can redirect student behaviour.				
I know how to conduct a risk assessment when anger erupts into violence.				
I know the law when anger erupts into violence.				
I can manage a recovery period.				
I can manage my own anger.				

Chapter 5
Do you understand manipulative anger?

The distinct forms of anger

There are two distinct forms of anger that are manifested in the classroom. The first – reactive anger – is relatively healthy: it happens, and is a normal part of being human. The second, manipulative anger is less so: it is anger with a 'high IQ', is proactive and is goal-driven.

You will come across both types in your classroom. Dealing with the former – reactive anger – though difficult, is entirely possible if you use some of the de-escalation techniques in this book. However, being dumped in a classroom where every single child is expressing manipulative anger towards the perceived outsider – which, in case you were wondering, is you – can make you want to quit the profession. It is displays of manipulative anger that will cause you the real problems, and it is well worth being versed in its various nuances for you to be successful in the challenging classroom.

Manipulative anger

In inter-group relationships, anger makes people think in more negative and prejudiced terms about outsiders. Anger makes people less trusting, and slower to attribute good qualities to outsiders.[1]

---

[1] DeSteno et al., 2004, pp. 319–24.

The point of any manipulative display of aggression in the classroom is to disempower the outsider – you – and there can be times in the truly difficult class that you will feel completely and utterly disempowered.

Stop press. You do not have to feel disempowered! You can take steps to ensure that you win most of the small battles; you'll lose some: you may lose many, but it is entirely possible for you to come out the other side having won the class's respect and, eventually, their devotion. But it is a case of understanding that you are in for many, many of these one-on-one battles of will. If you can come out of 60% of them having let students know that you are unfazed, that you are aware of their intentions and that your sole concern is for their achievement and well-being, then you'll win eventually.

Understanding that there are different forms of manipulative anger and recognizing which particular form you are in receipt of will help you to remain resolute in your understanding that you are witnessing pathological behaviour and that you must choose the most professional path of action to take. This chapter is designed to acquaint you with the various forms, how they manifest and what you can do to ensure you come out of each engagement with an (admittedly rueful) smile on your face.

Manipulative aggression is where anger is employed as a means of getting something. This 'something' can be money, girlfriends or boyfriends, status, or a possession owned by another person. Regardless, the aggressive instincts are actively engaged to get the desired 'something'.

In a classroom, most likely, it will be about gaining power and status. The intent of manipulative aggression in a classroom is to steal these two commodities from the teacher.

As a classroom teacher you are very likely to be in receipt of a version of this aggression when taking your first few classes in a challenging school. Students in such environments will be initially hostile to any new teacher (it is not about you – it just feels like it is). They may well be used to behaving in the manner they see fit, ignoring anything that might be termed reasonable behaviour. They may well even have had a string of supply teachers before you, for whom they displayed little respect. You waltzing into a room that they regard as owning themselves and attempting to put order on to their chaos is an explicit threat to their territory and they will seek to undermine you.

The ways in which they will attempt to do this are manifold, but are substantially less sophisticated than they might originally seem. Students will challenge every single thing that you do; in every interaction you have with them, they will actively seek to subvert the general order, so that they are the boss and you are left feeling what they regard you as: an offensive intruder.

The desired result is to make you go away; to see you lose it; for you to shout, or to make a professional error that they feel justified in making a complaint about to the headteacher. It is very important that you don't fall prey to their attempts and instead employ the techniques that we will discuss later in this chapter.

We will now go through the different behaviours you might experience in the classroom and how you should respond to them. You might not initially recognize all of these as being versions of manipulative aggression, but they are and it is helpful to understand the full array to equip you with the knowledge and skills to tackle challenging behaviour in as effective manner as possible.

Threats

Specifically, these will relate to your career. 'I could have you sacked for that', or, 'I am tempted to inform my mother of your actions here, and she will be most displeased, as she is a personal friend of the headteacher.' It is plausible, also, that you might be threatened with physical violence: 'If you don't get out of my face, I am going to hit you!' Being in receipt of such a threat for the first time from a young person you are trying to help can be extremely shocking, and may instantly cause you to think ill of them. Remember in this situation the cardinal rule. Do not let their behaviour affect your attitude!

How to respond

There is little point attempting to rationalize in this situation. One successful way of dealing with such threats is to treat them with a degree of mock serious gravitas, and to get students to write them down. Telling them, 'You are entirely welcome to make a complaint about my behaviour. However, it will be taken more seriously if you put it in writing. Here is a pen. You may need to redraft it! Have I taught you the generic conventions of a letter of complaint, yet?'

You may choose to tactically ignore the behaviour and redirect the student to the piece of work that they are meant to be doing. Your response to, 'I am going to hit you' is, therefore, to ignore it and say, 'Yeh, but what about this piece of work you're doing here?' Whatever decision you make about the immediate management of the incident, you must write it down and pass your log of the incident to a senior manager. Threatening people who are there to help is a poor habit for a student to get into and some punitive action will have to be taken, though it may be, because of the severity of the offence, that it is taken at a higher level than you are at in terms of professional status.

Hurtfulness

You may well be verbally abused because of your appearance, your demeanour, or anything about you that does not meet with perversely socialized forms of acceptability. This may involve language that you find beyond the pale. We, the authors, have been described as mad and ugly, have been told that we look like junkies, and that our coat looked as if it came from a junk shop.[2] Students will also attempt to blame you for everything that goes wrong in the class, and many is the time you will be in receipt of the accusation that, 'You aren't controlling us.' Your own feelings will be deliberately placed on a rack, and students will push you as far as they can to see what you are made of. There is a marvellous line by the poet, Charles Bukowski, in the poem *The Genius of the Crowd*. He writes:

Beware those who seek constant crowds for
they are nothing alone
Beware the average man the average woman
Beware their love, their love is average
seeks average
but there is genius in their hatred[3]

And there will be times when you will be greeted with the full genius of their hatred.

How to respond

Remember: you are being insulted by a 13-year-old. Water. Duck. Back.

---

[2] The fact that this is true doesn't make it any less hurtful.
[3] Bukowski, 1966.

Take it in, and use it as ammunition for a display of self-deprecatory humour, for example: 'Yeh, I know, even my mum thinks I'm ugly … but what am I to do? I can't afford a facelift. Do you know how little they pay me?'

However, if the incident is such that you cannot laugh it off, then you must write it down and inform the student that there must be a consequence for stepping over the mark. It is about locating the intent. If you think the comment was merely an accident, and the student was not seeking to hurt you, then you moderate your own reaction and laugh it off. If it was targeted at you with intent, then take action.

Destructiveness

The destruction of objects, their own work, or the work of others seems to be the least sane of any of the possible aggressive responses to a teacher; you might well wonder why someone would bother to destroy their own efforts. In the truly challenging classroom, however, there will often be a perverse, negative, oppositional attitude to creativity. You will often experience individual students tearing pages out of their books, or screwing up their work and chucking it across the room if you make anything that might even be perceived as a borderline negative comment about it. Negative, in this arena, might include being caught saying, 'This is fantastic, Lou.' The screwing up of work here is a deliberate, manipulative tactic and should be recognized and treated as such.

How to respond

First, no one is ever to think that they are allowed to tear out a page from a book without your assistance; if a page must be torn out, it is only to be the teacher who does it. If a student is excessively negative about their own work in order to manipulate you into an adverse reaction, then you merely react constructively. If a student has destroyed some of their work, save what you can – calmly, take the paper from the corner of the room, unfold it, sit next to the young person and say what was good about the work, explaining that it was a good start, and that you were really pleased with it, that the student would probably benefit from transcribing it on a fresh page in their exercise book, and, from then, extending on the great start that has been made.

Bullying

Bullying constitutes pushing, shoving, shouting, or any attempt at playing on weakness. When it comes to child-on-child bullying, the response you must have is unequivocal: you must be totally and utterly intolerant of it. It is unacceptable for one person in the class to use bullying to suggest that they are better than someone else in the class, and your best response in this situation is to make your understanding of this explicit. The question, 'Do you think you are better than Shannon?' generally shame-faces the offending student into acknowledging that they are not better than Shannon, and should not continue to think that discriminating or bullying another human in the class is a decent way of going about business.

Where the bullying is directed at you, you must remember that you are the grown-up in the room and that you must attempt – at least – to not let it hit the child in you. However, be aware that, as much as we – all of us – might look something like proper grown-ups, we aren't always the idealized version of ourselves that we would perhaps wish to be.

In the most challenging environments you will find whole classes who manage to find your Achilles' heel and poke at it stubbornly and repeatedly with a sharp stick, to see what might happen. This is 'class-on-teacher' bullying and it is very hard to deal with indeed. You might have a particularly difficult relationship with the fact that some stupid people called you ugly when you were a child; your financial struggles might be reflected a little too obviously in the threads you wear to work; you may currently be struggling with the idea that you are 'unboyfriendable'. Whatever your most pronounced personal issue is, be assured that certain classes are likely to have a sonar with which they will be able to detect it.

How to respond

Don't wince when they manage to hit you where it hurts! Think of the cricketer, Brian Close, who was famed for taking the full force of the most hostile West Indies' attack of all time on his unprotected body and would not even so much as flinch. If you give the class the indication that they have hurt you, then they will merely send more bouncers into that particular territory. Here, again, the reflective surface of the smile becomes the Teflon that you use to ensure that the students are unable to locate that the sweet spot has been hit.

Unjust blaming

You are there to help them, to aid their path into a profitable and functional adulthood. It is difficult to fathom why, oh why, they are blaming you for everything that goes wrong, when it would be clear, to any rational human being, that none of the stuff that is going wrong in the life of your class is in any way your fault. You will be told that your instructions were insufficiently clear, when they were abundantly so; you will be informed by Pip that you allowed Charlene to do, last week, just the very thing that you are upbraiding Pip for this week; you will be informed loudly and publicly that you are not managing the class properly, and that it is all your fault that they are displaying every, single, distinct pathology of manipulatively aggressive behaviour!

How to respond

Thankfully, this stage doesn't actually play out for too long; it is very much an early-stage part of the process of winning over the difficult class. You might think it worth engaging with and rationalizing it out with the student who is blaming you; but it's not worth the bother and will land you in all kinds of trouble with secondaries.[4] A better approach, and one which puts the power back in your hands, is to ask the rhetorical question, 'Is that what you think?' before intoning, 'That's an interesting idea.' Shrug it off, redirect, or just move on.

Grandiosity

Grand displays of quite absurd public behaviour can happen quite often in the early days with the truly difficult class. These can range from a mild bit of forgivable showing-off, to standing in front of the class and doing a 'fat-bum movement ballet' while singing a procession of the most profane words in the style of an opera singer, all while you are trying to teach. The daftness of these behaviours can be off-putting, or alarming, or amusing. In the first lesson with a new class, Phil was in mid-sentence, spelling out the learning objectives, when one of the students started singing – in September – the tune 'It's Beginning to Look a Lot Like Christmas'. As the rest of the

---

[4] Arguing with the way you are managing a situation rather than acknowledging the initial point.

class joined in, there was little possible response other than applauding at the end.

Not all displays of grandiosity are quite so charming though. And remember the intention of a display of grandiose behaviour is manipulative aggression: it is to destroy your ability to manage the class. Any attempt to steal centre-stage from you is an attempt to undermine and subtly humiliate you.

How to respond

It is difficult to be upstaged if you have a well-planned and agreed seating plan. However, if, despite this, a student wants to steal the spotlight, you will find that you will not be humiliated if you do not allow yourself to appear humiliated. The answer with the most extreme and silly forms of spotlight grabbing is to stand at the side and let it play out, with a wry smile. Rarely will the person who has stolen the class's attention know what to do with it, and both class and performer will get bored quickly enough. Once it has played out, take the appropriate action, but do it calmly. It may be that you just ask the student to go outside to consider how they might improve the performance next time, or that you calmly request senior management to come and take the young actor away. Once the student has been dispensed with, you then talk to the rest of the class, stating that as much as you enjoyed the performance it was inappropriate behaviour for a learning environment, and that there must sadly (as you very much like the student in question) be a consequence for such an incident.

This is always a good technique when you are in a challenging situation with any one member (or members) of a difficult class. After the incident has occurred and you have calmly taken whatever action is appropriate to secure a consequence, you then express love for the young person to the rest of the class and then spell out what the consequences for the behaviour will be. It lets the class know that you are unruffled by displays of poor behaviour, that you are there for them and for their learning, and that there will always be a consequence.

The key is to remain unruffled. With the less wild and more common displays of grandiosity, you should just point them back in the direction of the learning. Say, for example: 'We have a rule in this class that there is to be only one person speaking at a time; it is a rule we have all agreed on, as it is in the behaviour policy, and your behaviour in speaking over me is stopping us from learning.'

Vengefulness

There is a rule of thumb in schools: students get a fresh slate in the morning. Ordinarily, whatever has happened the day before will be forgotten the next day, and everyone starts again, relatively happily. However, there will be the odd occasion that something has occurred from which the fallout lasts a little longer, and there will be a child who is not prepared to forget a particular slight, imagined or real.

On the very rare occasion that a student is vengeful towards you, it will be as a result of you having, as they would put it, 'Got them into trouble.' And this vengefulness will take the form of profane insults about your person, muttered or aloud. In one instance, Phil had a particularly unhappy boy in his class; let's call him Jim, though this is not his name. Jim had experienced an unending oasis of pure naughtiness in one particular lesson and Phil decided that the appropriate consequence would be to prevent Jim from being involved in football training, of which Jim was most fond, that particular evening. Having made the agreement with the PE teacher, Phil informed Jim of the decision. Jim was most displeased. He decided that his conduct in future, on ever encountering Phil, would be to spit out the words, 'You queer!' Despite Phil's exhortations that this was, perhaps, not the way to speak to a graduate professional who is in *loco parentis*, the phrase and course of action amused Jim so much that he persisted with it, for months. Every interaction went along the following lines:

Teacher: Good morning, Jim.

Jim: Piss off, you poof.

Teacher: Okay. Could you desist from that language before you enter the classroom.

Jim: Queer.

Teacher: I will have to have you taken away by senior management if you continue.

Jim: Go on then, you queer. See if I care. (*Jim is escorted away – all the while shouting*) You poof. You queer. You queer! You queer poofy queer poof!

How to respond

Now, it is difficult to discern the correct professional path of action when confronted with the vengefulness of the nature that Jim displayed. It is likely in such an extreme case, as was the case with Jim, that one day he just won't be there any more, as the school will have found alternative provision for him.

However, the knowledge that this will eventually happen will not make it much easier for you while you are experiencing it, and you will probably find that the best course of action is to call a conference with Jim's parents or carers, to give them choices of how to bring their child back from the brink and avoid exclusion.

Unpredictability

This can be quite a serious challenge in the early days of managing a difficult class and it is best to go in knowing that you will often find yourself dealing with a variety of extremes of illogic. In one particular school in which we both worked, the technique of baffling with blinding illogic was often employed. At the start of one lesson, one of the girls, when greeted at the door by her teacher with the requisite smile, turned away saying, 'Oh no. Not this f***ing idiot again' and refused to enter the lesson. In the space of the same long hour, a different girl, piped up, 'You ain't teaching us nuffink!' Even calm reference to the lesson objectives didn't work, as it was greeted with the emphatic statement, 'I *is* entitled to my own opinion!'[5]

Many students will employ the 'going off the handle for nothing at all' technique, either with you, or more likely with a classmate, who may be complicit in the ruse. It is a favoured tactic of the bored, serial work avoider.

How to respond

The natural reaction is to hit the negative with a negative. This doesn't work and will encourage things to escalate. Restate your intention and inform the student that you will happily discuss in private whether they are learning anything from your lesson after the end of the lesson. Say, for example:

---

[5] 'And will be even more so entitled if I learn how to properly conjugate the verb "to be".'

'Let's sit together and see if I can work out a way of making the lesson better for you.'

When a student is 'flying off the handle' for no reason, make sure you employ the body language used in conflict situations, as explained in Chapter 3.

Passive anger

Passive expressions of manipulative anger are less obviously confrontational by nature, and often all the more insidious and scary as a result. The intent behind most passively expressed forms of anger is to get inside your head and to ruin either your confidence or your standing with either the rest of the class or with your colleagues.

Some of the behaviours discussed below are truly awful, but we would not be doing our jobs as authors of this book if we attempted to hide them. When you experience passive anger in one of its various forms, then your vision of what constitutes humanity may well take a sharp turn towards the negative. Your job is to get to the bottom of it. Bear in mind that there is bound to be a backstory that is the context for a student's frustrated anger, possibly to do with their lack of progress; they may be aware that they have not had good teaching in the past (before you) and may have lost the will to study. The only person present for them to blame is you. There is no one else to take the flak.

Secretive behaviour

There may be a student in the class who does not seem to dislike you, and to whom you will occasionally turn when things are cutting up rough. You may then find out that this very student is actually at the centre of things, and is providing much of the ammunition for the others to use. This can cause a crucifying loss of confidence, for a new teacher in particular. On these occasions, when you feel that you have been betrayed by a student, try to remember they are just a child and that everyone makes mistakes. Be sorry for them that they are not able to conduct relationships with a degree of trust yet, and hope that, one day, the student will learn this lesson.

Related to this form of passive anger, is a student gossiping about you, making anonymous complaints or writing poison pen letters. If you do receive any of the latter, then you must show the evidence immediately to your manager.

What you will almost certainly come across is the muttered comment underneath the breath: this is a much-favoured technique of students in challenging schools. Its intent is to take away your status and your authority, and it will be done with a technician's expertise in pitching it at just the right level so that it is recognizable – to you and the class – that something has been said, but that you will not have heard the exact words.

The muttered comment will ordinarily come at the end of whatever discussion you are having with the student, when the student feels somehow slighted by the content or the tone of that discussion. If, for whatever reason, they feel that they have lost face in front of their friends, then they will take back that status. The muttered comment, for example, 'Yeh, shut up, you idiot', will be used to put the student back on top in terms of status in front of their mates.

The key is not to put yourself in the position that you have altered the student's status in front of their mates, by having whatever conversation you need to in private. Away from the eyes and ears of the rest of the class, most students are perfectly personable and able to see reason. Speak to them reasonably: ask them to remember that you are a human being and not just a teacher, and that you only want the best for them.

However, if you are in a situation where you have just about caught the tail end of a muttered response, there is a correct way and an incorrect way to deal with it.

How to respond

With the muttered comment under the breath, you must *call them up on each one you think you hear.* Use firm eye contact and say: 'If you've got something to say, could you say it louder, please?' This expressed rhetorically works well. Alternatively, sit beside the student and quietly, and non-confrontationally, using a friendly facial expression and tone, ask what they said.

As you will not have heard exactly what the student did say, attempting to repeat it back to them does not work. Getting it even slightly wrong will just confirm that you haven't heard correctly and that the student can continue with the technique. If you ask the young person what they said, then you are playing into their hands in terms of who has the status in the transaction. The student will respond that they did not say anything and this will play out in front of the class. There is no way of winning in this situation, and you are just digging a bigger hole for yourself.

You will probably experience this form of behaviour multiple times, even if you challenge it correctly (particularly if you are in any way short of perfect hearing – in which case students will have all sorts of fun and japery with it). If you let the comment go unchallenged, however, then you are giving permission for it to continue, and you should never, even unintentionally, give permission for poor behaviour.

Psychological manipulation

The manifestations of this are manifold within the difficult classroom and, again, the main aim of it is to strip you of your status as a professional in front of an audience. One of the key manifestations of psychological manipulation is to provoke you to anger and then patronize you for having expressed that anger.

There will be times whilst enduring the drip-drip-drip of manipulative behaviour that you feel yourself about to lose it, and then you will be tempted to shout. Don't! This is exactly what the class that is experienced in challenging and manipulating teachers is hoping for, and there will always be a follow-up slam dunk answer when they manage to drive you to shouting, which is the indignantly expressed line, something along the lines of, 'Why are you shouting at us for?' The grammatical construction of this question only makes it more absurdly humiliating: you are being challenged on your behaviour by outrageously behaved young people who cannot even construct a grammatical sentence! But, if they are able to dispense the summary justice that this line implies, it will have been your fault. You gave it to them.

How to respond

To get a real sense of what it is like to be shouted at by a teacher go into the bathroom, put your face up to the mirror and shout at it. There you go: you look ugly and you're covered in spit. Don't do this to children. In addition, it is almost impossible to construct a coherent sentence when you are shouting. You can't communicate properly if you are shouting; therefore, as communication is the bedrock of teaching, you are not being a teacher in any positive meaning of the word.

If any of the forms of psychological manipulation are designed to take away your professional status, then it is simple: don't let them. Don't behave in the way that they are attempting to make you behave. Be a professional.

If the intent of the behaviour is to make you shout, then don't shout. Professional teachers generally don't need to. It doesn't do much for you. It will get the class's attention, albeit briefly, but shouting at students is not what good teachers do, and shouting at any one particular child is actually really quite damaging for the child: it is possible they may well get enough of this at home.

Sexual provocation

The most frightening and disturbing of any of the forms of psychological manipulation you will encounter will be sexual provocation. This stomach-churning behaviour is thankfully rare; but we are living in an age where young people are sexualized at an increasingly early age and, heartbreak-ingly, there are young people for whom the only real validation they ever get to experience is as a result of what others – specifically people older than them – convey to them in the way of glances, comments or worse.

At certain ages, flirting at your teacher is a pretty sweet and normal part of growing up, and it could be postulated that actually there is (or, at least, should be) no safer place than to make your first clumsy attempts at experi-menting with the earliest versions of your nascent sexuality than with a professional who really cares about your well-being and would not dream of ever stealing anything from you. Most suggestive behaviour from student to teacher is therefore the utterly innocent flowering of a bud into the direction of being a blossom.

Sadly, though, it isn't always thus. There are young people who believe that they can use their physicality as a tool with which to manipulate others. Be very sad for them that someone has taught them this lesson. But if it is directed at you, then you have been dunked into very murky territory without your permission and, once you are certain that what is being directed at you is not innocent, then you must have sufficient compassion for the young person displaying the behaviour to find help for them.

How to respond

If you suspect any form of sexual provocation, then you must write down exactly what happened. Do not express an opinion – just relate the facts – and hand this to a member of senior management. If a child is expressing themselves in a provocative manner to a teacher, then it may be that the child requires help and this has to be done through the correct agencies. If the child does not need help, the fact that you have run their behaviour immediately through quite serious channels may be sufficiently heavy a message for it not to occur again.

Self-blame or ineffectualness

Being useless can actually be a deliberate, manipulative form of passive aggression. You will experience this behaviour most in the early stages of your relationship with a difficult class. Students may use negative expressions about themselves, for example: 'I'm rubbish at this subject.' 'Sorry, I can't do this.' 'I can't do essays.' 'I don't understand this subject.'

The ploy with this negative self-talk is to trap you into agreeing with them, and then to be livid with your response. 'You're supposed to be encouraging us, not telling us we're rubbish!' This ploy is designed to make things stay as they are. Students in a difficult class do want to achieve but they will fight against all of the changes that they must make in order for them to achieve. Expressing negativity about their work or their abilities is a device that is designed to stop them from embracing the innate difficulties of optimism. As we looked at previously, an optimist is someone who believes it is their own fault if something is not working – that way they can do something about it – they can self-examine their actions and change. Someone stuck in a cycle of negativity will not want to make this change and will simply blame their perceived innate lack of ability on the fact that an external factor isn't working. Furthermore, to be optimistic and to attempt to achieve is to risk failure. In the mind of the challenging class, failure is okay if it is comfortable, and the students are used to it. The failure that involves effort which does not meet a reward is the failure that they fear; as it will completely condemn them to living without the excuse, 'I could have done it if I could have been bothered.'

The 'comfort zone' is called that because it is a comfortable place in which to live; if students remain in it they can maintain a comfortable image of themselves. They are scared to go into a different zone where their image of themselves may be forced to change. Learning is an emotional process that requires the learner to admit deficiencies, and none of us are too keen on doing this.

Consequently, you will be greeted with a lot of negatively expressed self-talk at the beginning of your relationship with a difficult class. It is your job to turn this into expressions of optimistic positivity.

Occasionally, negative talk will combine with various forms of subconsciously deliberate ineffectualness: never having a pen; 'accidentally' breaking whatever writing implement they have with them; expressing frustration at utterly insignificant things while ignoring serious ones.

You may also come across another version of subconsciously deliberate ineffectualness: the over-obsession with presentation to the exclusion of all else, or the obsession with correctness. This is a combination of a mild display of obsessive compulsive disorder (OCD) with a more deliberate act of self-focused negativity, which is little more than an advanced version of a work avoidance technique. Any diagnostic comment you make about the work of a student will result in the student tearing the page out of the book, or scribbling through it. This appears to be a particularly pointless act of self-sabotage at first, and indeed it is, but it is also an act, the intent of which is to rubbish (literally) the comments you have made to help them move on, to change, to improve. In this, it is the close cousin of the negative self-talk: it is a display of learned helplessness, and its intent is for you to leave them alone to stew in their depression, or to do their work for them. Neither path is acceptable.

How to respond

These situations require you to have the patience of either a saint, a nun or of Job.[6]

You must remember you are the professional, and part of your professionalism is the fact that you are prepared for self-blame, ineffectualness and self-defeating perfectionism. As the professional you are aware that all of these are strategies (albeit unconscious ones), and that they are early-stage

---

[6] A righteous man whom Satan convinces God to let him torment: kills his kids, destroys his livestock, gives him boils, all in order to tempt Job into saying something a bit off about God. Which he does.

strategies. If you respond correctly you will not see these behaviours very much after the first few weeks. You must be firm, yet understanding, and be convincing in your responses. Remain unremittingly positive. Repeat the mantra, 'You can do it. I believe in you.' Look the student in the eyes while you are saying this. If your suggestions for improvement are taken negatively, tell the student that it is not your job to let them stay as they are: it is to move them forward, and the way of moving forward is to make small changes.

Above all, reassure the young person that you are interested in them and in their work and that you are there for their learning. This stage will have blown over by the beginning of the first half-term break.

Why is failure good?

A famous man once said that the secret to his considerable success was a phenomenal appetite for failure. This appetite was, in fact, his chief secret: his success was predicated on being knocked out again and again by progressively bigger opponents. The authors of this book nod at their betters, and acknowledge that whatever paltry achievements we have made are a result of biting off a piece that was clearly far too big for us, and getting down to some serious and focused chewing.

It can be difficult to pass on the importance of this mindset to students who fear, above all things, failure. It may be that they have learnt from a young age that failure is to be avoided at all costs. If you are to win the rewards your class need, then you must try to reinforce the message to your students that failure is not the enemy of learning. And learning is their goal. This is a mindset that must become engrained early on.

Dispassion

Dispassion, as is intended, can be infuriating. It is an array of milk-curdling and phoney smiles and shrugs; the expression 'Uh-uh-uh!' (which is teenage for 'I don't know', 'I don't care', 'I've given up caring'); allowing others to sort things out, and deliberately remaining completely passive when confronted with another's anger or concern.

This is a passive aggressive technique employed largely to infuriate, to put you in a position where you are likely to lose control. It is plausible that someone who is not professionally trained might indeed lose control. You are professionally trained. Don't give the behaviour the reward it seeks.

The cousin of this technique, in terms of levels of audibility, is the silent treatment. You will attempt to rationalize a situation or a piece of conflict with the student; they will point-blank refuse to say anything at all – and their tenacity in not saying anything at all is not to be questioned. The silence will be accompanied by the avoidance of eye contact. This is a learned technique, though you would be well advised to understand that there are specific cultural issues here. In some cultures, avoiding eye contact with the elder is a sign of deference, and you saying, 'Look me in the eyes when I am speaking to you' is utterly misunderstanding the behaviour: you are mistaking deference for insolence, and, in doing so, confusing the child as much as you are confusing yourself.

In some instances this deliberate and wilful evasion tactic mutates into the body language you might expect from a six-year-old. The student's display of dispassion may move beyond passively refusing to engage in any dialogue with you. They will not merely refuse to engage or to argue back, but will turn their back to you as you are talking to them; perhaps even disappear under a table and curl up into a ball.

How to respond

There is not much you can do here. Even if you remain preternaturally rational on the outside (you will struggle to remain so on the inside), you will probably get no response from the student. Your best bet is to park the problem and come back to it. Write it down and refer the student on to someone else. Remember, though, you are the one making the decision. Like a tactical retreat in battle: you are not actually giving up on the battle itself.

Test yourself

	Very confident	Confident	Not confident	Huh?
Do you understand manipulative anger?				
I am aware of the difference between reactive and manipulative anger.				
I have strategies to deal with threats.				
I have strategies to deal with destructiveness.				
I have strategies to deal with bullying.				
I have strategies to deal with unjust blaming.				
I have strategies to deal with grandiosity.				
I have strategies to deal with vengefulness.				
I have strategies to deal with unpredictability.				
I know how passive anger manifests.				
I have strategies to deal with secretive behaviour.				

I have strategies to deal with psychological manipulation.				
I have strategies to deal with self-blame.				
I have strategies to deal with dispassionate behaviour.				

Chapter 6
Can you use de-escalation techniques?

If you recognize that a student is entering the arousal stage of anger, you will want to be in possession of a full range of techniques to circumvent the situation, and lead both student and class back safely towards the path of calm. As we saw in Chapter 4 there are a few available routes you may wish to take: these include redirection, diffusion and containment.

These de-escalation techniques are generally to be used as proactively as possible, so that the crisis stage of an incident is averted. However, many of them can also be applied during or after the crisis stage with equal efficacy. It is very important to act quickly, be decisive, pick a technique and put it into action straightway. Most of the time, to a greater or lesser degree, one of these techniques will resolve the situation before it gets too aggravated, and before blows or foul curses are exchanged.

Before we describe the different de-escalation techniques you can employ, you must first come to the understanding that humour is always, in all circumstances, the most effective solution. This may seem unlikely, but, for a moment...

Imagine yourself being really quite angry about something. Think of one of your triggers and see if you can think yourself into a state of anger.

Now imagine yourself being tickled.

Imagine yourself trying – desperately – to stay angry while being tickled.

And realize it would be very difficult to maintain such a focus on your purple rage when being tickled: it would alter your chemistry and destroy the anger's ability to remain sharp.

Laughter utterly diffuses anger. You should already have an understanding that there is a sound neurobiological reason behind this; as we described earlier, laughter is the body's way of dealing with relief, when an anticipated episode of mortal danger does not result in damage. In making a student laugh at a time when they are angry, you are short-circuiting the body's systems of protection into the state that comes after a happy resolution to a threatening episode; you are fast-forwarding the body into believing it is all over, and your student will behave accordingly.

There are times when humour as a diffusion tactic can be high risk, and there will be times when you get it very wrong However, a light-hearted teacher who is able to laugh at themselves publicly is often the teacher who is most easily able to break down barriers of status and is, accordingly, the most able to act effectively to diffuse incidents before they occur.

Over the next few pages, we aim to give you a full range of de-escalation techniques that you can reach for to prevent the build-up stage of a student's anger ever getting the chance to metamorphose into full-blown anger.

De-escalation technique 1: Standing between the combatants

This is a no brainer. If two students are entering into the murky waters that might, if unchecked, burst into physical violence, real or play – remember, the latter easily mutates into the former – then you should immediately stand in the space between them. You stand at a point that is equidistant from the combatants, and in order to break their eye-line. If they are unable to see each other they will soon get bored of the game, and will hopefully start to focus back on their work. If they are set on causing physical harm to each other, then, in order to do so, they would have to knock you over, and even in the most challenging schools, students will give this a second thought, and will generally give it up as a mug's game.

De-escalation technique 2: Swapping out

Chuck your ego in the bin. It is doing you no good. Show the requisite humility: ask your colleague for help. It doesn't matter if you don't like them. It doesn't matter if they are less experienced than you. It is not a professional embarrassment asking them for assistance. Ask them for help. It is a collegiate profession: they'll respond. It may be that you think they are actually nowhere as good a teacher as you. It may be that you don't agree with some of their attitudes or techniques; it doesn't matter. Ask for help.

It is quite possible that they will have a better relationship with the particular student than you, and that, in asking your colleague to look after the student for the rest of the lesson, you will be able to teach the rest of the class without damaging your mental and physical health. Ask your colleague to take the student into their class. You will also find that there will be students who they teach with whom you have a better relationship than they do, and that you will sometimes have to look after a student they are struggling with. This is a reciprocal arrangement that helps both of you. Don't see this action as an expression of failure: you are applying a strategy that is focused on the needs of all the learners, and are differentiating your behaviour management. If another teacher is better able to manage the demands the student is currently making on you, then differentiate, especially if you feel your own arousal being triggered.

De-escalation technique 3: Model the behaviour you want the student to adopt

One of the issues you may find confusing, especially when you are first starting out, is that sometimes students – genuinely, honestly – don't actually know how to behave. Remember, childhood and school exists to socialize children, to introduce them to accepted social norms. Children are still at the nascent stage of learning those norms, and it may be what you expect your students to do is something that they have never been taught to do before. The solution is to teach them, by modelling how to do it.

Take, for instance, a student who is rocking on their chair. It may sound ludicrous to you, but the problem could be that they just don't know how to sit on a chair without rocking on it. Perhaps the student's whole family is comprised of inveterate chair rockers, and that balancing on the back two legs of the chair is a social norm where they live.

'Pass the beans, love.'

'I can't reach them.'

The formula here is simple: you – teach – model – explain – role-play. See it as a miniscule, four-part lesson: you start by telling the student you are going to teach them how to sit properly on their chair, then demonstrate how to do it. Having demonstrated, you talk through how exactly you went about achieving the Herculean task of sitting on a chair without rocking, delve into the technical aspects of it, then ask them to perform the same action all the while giving them feedback on it.

The same applies with any example of bad behaviour, from interrupting to constantly clicking a pen when you are speaking. Teach the student how not to do it, demonstrate how not to do it, talk through how you stopped yourself from doing it, and get the young person to practise not doing it. This way you avoid the student (or yourself) from even getting into the arousal zone. Imagine if you genuinely didn't know how to stop doing something and a teacher continually told you that you had to. You'd be confused and slightly humiliated. This technique stops all that unpleasantness from occurring.

De-escalation technique 4: Change the activity/location

If a student is entering the build-up phase of anger, it may be that it is the activity they are undertaking that is causing the stress which will result in a display of reactive anger. Imagine a student who has a speech impediment. You have asked them to present to the class and it is causing them to enter an unremitting inferno of absolute stress. A clever teacher, on noticing the first signs of arousal, would rapidly change the activity, or the requirements placed on that particular student: they'd ask them to take written notes on the performance of everybody else rather than delivering themselves.

Another useful technique, if stress is building in a student, is to ask them to go for a quick walk along the corridor (with a note, of course) and to come back in two minutes. By briefly and decisively altering the stimulus they are in receipt of, you are taking away the immediate trigger, and the student may well return, calmed and ready to face the demands of the classroom with new verve.

In certain circumstances it may be necessary, or helpful, to accompany the student. If you are witnessing a potential incident arising in the corridors, for instance, it can be really useful just to ask one of the students involved to follow you, and to go for a walk around the school, perhaps on some made-up errand. Stride purposefully and energetically, as the physical aspect of the walk burns off some of the student's energy and adrenalin. Get the student to follow you, and note that, after a minute or so of walking in any direction, you can discuss the situation sensibly, perhaps employing the CUDSA technique (see page 63) to agree how to resolve the situation to everyone's satisfaction.

De-escalation technique 5: Praise recent positives

This is another good technique to use when it appears that the task is the trigger. If a student is entering either learnt or real helplessness when presented with a task, and you have pretty good reason to believe that this could escalate, you nip their growing feelings of arousal in the bud by scaffolding the young person with positive language. Refer to a recent achievement the student has made, or a time when they did a good piece of work, and make a specific comment on how well they did, suggesting the same can be achieved this time. You might say something along the lines of:

> *Remember last week, when you did that fantastic piece of work on ox-bow lakes. You started off just by doing a couple of lines, and it ended up as one of the best pieces of work in the class. Try that again. Let me know if it's working in five minutes.*

There is a related technique that can work very well with students who find their emotional life difficult to manage, and that is to remind them of a time when they managed their behaviour during a recent event. When you notice that the student's anger has been triggered, say, for example, 'I can see that you are getting angry. Remember last week when you took a walk outside, thought about how much you love your dog, and then returned ready for work. I'll write you a note.'

Here we give attainable, short targets; the success this technique can have with the most troubled of students is marked.

De-escalation technique 6: Be silent

This is a useful crisis-stage technique when a student is really very cross indeed. You remain completely silent until they have calmed down. You do this in order to give the young person the space to work things out for themselves. The technique relies on there being sufficient time for their emotion to play out, and, bearing in mind that it can take anger about 45 minutes to dissipate, you may not have enough time available. But if a student is to be allowed to articulate what it is they want to do, or be done, about the situation, they must be given the space to do this.

It is particularly useful to remain silent when a student has completely lost it. They kick the door. You stand there, silent, and watch them do it. They spit on the floor (near your feet). You look at the spit, but you don't say anything. They swear at you. You stand there. They swear at you again. No response. They say a naughtier swear word. You remain impassive. Eventually, as the adrenalin wears off, the student begins to feel a bit silly, begins to feel slightly penitent, slightly absurd. At this point the job is nigh on won and you can start guiding the young person, through a masterful use of the CUDSA technique to a resolution (see page 63).

De-escalation technique 7: Refer to attainable boundaries

The Boys' Achievement expert Gary Wilson refers to 'chunking things down'[1] for boys. This is a behavioural management technique that involves chunking your expectations down. If you are in a situation that is escalating and your best Leslie Phillips impersonation, combined with the instruction, 'Oh, do behave!' isn't having the desired effect, it could be because you are asking too much, and that the request is not easily attainable for the student. 'Oh, do behave' implies a whole series of instructions or conformities are in place. Remember, you are dealing with children, and it is entirely plausible that they don't understand exactly what they have to do in order to do what the teacher wants, so break it down into stages, preferably stages that come

---

[1] Wilson, 2006, p. 32.

with a time limit: 'In the next five minutes I would like you to have written to this point on the page.' 'The next thing I would like you to do is to put your pen on the table.' 'In 30 seconds I am going to check whether you have managed to do your top button up, and then I am going to go the full fascist and within a minute and a half I desire you to have also done your tie up.'

When a student is giving off all the signs of being work-shy, and is failing to do the work that you have set them, a fabulous technique is to put a mark on the page that you want the student to have written to before you will allow them to leave the room. Be steely about this and it will focus their mind fairly sharpish in order to get out to break or lunch on time.

De-escalation technique 8:
Reduce and extend personal space as appropriate

Judge the student's level of arousal and extend the personal space as necessary. As a rule of thumb, the more cross they are, the more space you need to give them. Get out of the way, the kettle's boiling!

After the incident, however, the student's key need is to know that everything is okay. A consoling hand on the shoulder can provide the reassurance required that whatever bridges have been unconsciously vandalized during the incident can be rebuilt.

De-escalation technique 9:
Let the student get on with it!

You've done the maths. You've done the risk assessment. The student has stormed out of the class. So what? You know the young person well, and, historically, when they are cross they go off and let off steam, and then come back and restart their work when they are in a better place. Let them get on with it.

De-escalation technique 10:
Ignore their behaviour altogether and praise the person next to them

No further explanation needed.

De-escalation technique 11:
Guide the student away physically

This is dependent on your existing relationship with the student. If you do not have an existing relationship of trust and mutual respect and liking, then do *not* do this: it will blow up in your face very badly! So the first thing you must do before attempting this technique is to perform the brief mental risk assessment by asking yourself the question, 'Do I have a sufficiently decent relationship with the student for them to trust me if I guide them away physically?' If the answer is yes (and don't do it if there is any doubt about the answer), then you, remembering all the time that the thumbs do the damage, place a hand on the shoulder, arm or elbow, and gently guide the student away from the incident, talking to them all the while you are doing so.

De-escalation technique 12:
Redirect the student

'Yeh, but what about that?' Point at it. Works like a charm. Anger is a sublimely solipsistic state: it doesn't recognize that it is feeding on its host. Merely pointing to something outside of the self and asking them to note it, can transport the angry student outside of themselves, so that they can pay attention, objectively, to the situation they are in at present.

Clearly the best thing to redirect the student towards is their work; but you can have fun with this one. As there is nigh on a foolproof guarantee you will get a result with this technique, you can play around with it. Saying, 'Yeh, but what about your work?' is great; but you can replace it with almost any noun: common or proper.

'Yeh, but what about my shoes?' will lead to the response, 'What about your shoes?' And the student will forget almost instantaneously that they were ever angry.

'Yeh, but what about the chickens?' has a pleasingly surreal edge.

'Yeh, but what about the little speck of dirt on this window … over here … come on … have a look!' redirects quite fully.

'Yeh, but what about the fact that I can't stop myself from walking like this?' accompanied by a silly walk brings the classroom mood back to the kind of area we might choose to inhabit.

De-escalation technique 13: Get a man in

Asking for assistance from another member of staff, or members, can be very useful support. There is a slightly odd statistical rule here though: where behaviour is escalating and only one student is involved, then the more staff you bring in, the more it will escalate, as the student will play up to the new audience. It's best with an individual to come up with an individual solution to the behaviour, one-on-one.

Where additional members of staff can be helpful is if you are dealing with a range of students. If a whole class is in an escalating state, bringing in members of staff as heavies pays off. A rule though, only one teacher should do the speaking. Agree who that is to be – preferably the class teacher who had responsibility for that class's achievement – and the other members of staff just stand there mute, like muscle-bound, gun-toting hoods, ensuring that the main teacher has a little bit of heavyweight insurance, *innit*.

De-escalation technique 14: Mirror the behaviour back in a humorous manner

This is a high-risk strategy and is not the kind of thing you would probably try in your NQT year, as you need to inhabit the skin of a teacher completely comfortably before you will be able to carry this off with any real chance of success. If you are confident enough it can diffuse a situation quite nicely:

where you are in receipt of some high-level behaviour, you mirror it back to the student with a ridiculous twist. A former colleague of ours, who is expert in working with children from the most challenging circumstances of all, when informed that a student was so cross that they were going to get a gun and kill him, would reply, 'Yeh, well I'm gonna kill you back.' Or if he was on the receiving end of naughty swearing would stand open-mouthed in mock outrage and ask, spluttering, 'Did you tell me to piss off? I can't believe you told me to piss off. That's a very bad swear word. It's actually the seventh baddest swear word in the whole list of really naughty words.'

De-escalation technique 15: Listen

We all want to be heard. Often you will find that the correct path through a behavioural incident comes not from doing, but by listening. If you listen, maintain open body language, all the time observing what the student's body language is telling you, that will help you pick up on verbal or visual cues which will tell you what the root of the problem is. Continue asking the same question, changing it only in minute increments, so that you go from, 'Unless you tell me the problem, I can't help', to 'I'm here to help you and you need to tell me what's wrong.' Eventually, the student will tell you and you can guide them to coming up with their own solution.

Test yourself

	Very confident	Confident	Not confident	Huh?
Can you use de-escalation techniques?				
I am aware that humour is the best de-escalation technique.				

I know how to stand between combatants.				
I have partnered up with another teacher to discuss behaviour management problems.				
I can model the behaviour I want to see.				
I am prepared to change the activity or location when an incident is in the build-up stage.				
I know how to praise recent positives.				
I am prepared to be silent during an incident.				
I set attainable boundaries.				
I extend or reduce personal space as appropriate.				
I am aware that it is sometimes appropriate to just 'let them get on with it'.				
I can use the 'ignore the behaviour and praise the person next to them' technique.				

I can judge when it is appropriate to guide a student away physically.				
I am aware of the dynamics of bringing other staff members into an incident.				
I am aware that 'mirroring behaviour' in a humorous manner can sometimes be effective.				
I listen.				

Chapter 7
Can you use humour to create relationships?

But do I have to be funny, boss? I'm not good at funny

As humans we have an array of basic needs that we want satisfied: sustenance, affection/sex and, of course, a swish pad in which to shelter from the ever-driving rain. It is arguable that we also have, as a basic human need, the need to laugh. There are people who have none of the preceding factors: neither food, nor wine, nor cuddles, nor sex, nor basic shelter; yet still they laugh.

We might argue that they are fools to do so. Or, alternatively, we might use this information to form an understanding that, of all the basic human needs, the most inviolable is the need to laugh. We can do so in the most unpleasant circumstances: the most lacerating grief can involve laughter. Indeed, laughter at one's fate can be a vital part of the process of forgetting, and many is the funeral oration that includes some fond humorous remembrance. The Dalai Lama, an authority on more or less everything, refers to his own response to the many tragedies his country has faced by saying that his chief response is laughter:

> I have been confronted with many difficulties throughout the course of my life, and my country is going through a critical period. But I laugh often, and my laughter is contagious. When people ask me how I find the strength to laugh now, I reply that I am a professional laugher.[1]

---

[1] Dalai Lama and Stril-Rever, 2010.

There is a sense that a teacher who wants to connect with his or her students in an empathetic way will, to some extent, also be a 'professional laugher'.

When we take CPD sessions, as a starter, we will ask delegates to get into pairs and ask one of the members of the pair to don a blindfold (which usually takes the form of one of the collection of manky, paisley, charity-shop ties one of the authors (Phil) has stored in a downstairs cupboard, beneath the rat poison). We will make the classroom or school hall into an assault course: upturned chairs, fake blood, gunpowder – you know the deal; and then ask the member of the pair who is not blindfolded to give the other directions as to how to get through the room without bumping into anything. Only these directions will be communicated through … a … drinking … straw.

And we learn exactly …?

Well …

Nothing really.

We have a laugh, though.

Which is well worth doing something for.

Because, in having a laugh, we reduce the distance between the people undertaking the activity. We realize that laughter is the smallest possible gap between two people, and that shared laughter causes us to bond with the people with whom we are sharing it.

Laughter is a connection that carries with it both compassion and empathy: in fact it is almost the definition of an empathetic state – to share a laugh you must be utterly in tune with someone, and with what they are feeling. It is a moment of symbiosis between two people, or between a person and a group of people: between teacher and class. The moment you are working with a challenging class and you are all laughing together is the moment you know that, even if you haven't got it entirely cracked just yet, you'll have it cracked soon.

Laughter takes away or obviates fear, particularly the fear of failure, and consequently it makes risk taking easier. Where in Chapter 5 we have written of the profound need for our students to embrace failure, it is entirely arguable that they will be more willing to do so after having had a right old laugh (at themselves).

The intention would be that we (all of us) should be running lessons that are at once deeply serious and profoundly light-hearted. If you think about it the notion of being light-hearted, when examined, is a reasonable encapsulation of everything we might want a teacher to be. 'Angels can fly,' says

G. K. Chesterton, 'because they take themselves lightly',[2] and in a tough school a teacher who carries a light heart is a teacher who can resolve the most heavyweight of issues without those issues ever becoming personalized, and who, in carrying that light heart, is able to give the child space in which to navigate. Laughter is, after all, perhaps the ultimate expression of safety.

Chesterton's equation of lightness with strength is philosophically diverting for a teacher in a challenging school, and excuse us if we dwell on it for a second. Chesterton writes:

> The swiftest things are the softest things. A bird is active, because a bird is soft. A stone is helpless, because a stone is hard. The stone must by its own nature go downwards, because hardness is weakness. The bird can of its nature go upwards, because fragility is force. In perfect force there is a kind of frivolity, an airiness that can maintain itself in the air.... Seriousness is not a virtue. It would be a heresy, but a much more sensible heresy, to say that seriousness is a vice. It is really a natural trend or lapse into taking one's self gravely, because it is the easiest thing to do. It is much easier to write a good *Times* leading article than a good joke in *Punch*. For solemnity flows out of men naturally; but laughter is a leap. It is easy to be heavy: hard to be light. Satan fell by the force of gravity.[3]

Use of self-deprecation

The taller and (at the time of writing) marginally balder of the two authors of this book is prone to introducing himself to either students or new colleagues in the following manner, 'I'm six-foot-four, totally bald and look like Shrek.' Given that he runs in the region of 20 schools, it might reasonably be concluded to be a poor résumé of his professional abilities. But it is an introduction that is used for a rationalized reason: it is used with an awareness that laughter breaks down barriers.

A teacher who finds themself able to be relaxed in being self-deprecatory is displaying that they are easy in the relationship they have with the class. Use of self-deprecatory humour is, therefore, counter-intuitively, a sign of

---

[2] Chesterton, 1908.
[3] Chesterton, 1908.

confidence: not just of the confidence the teacher has in themself, but also in the confidence they have in their relationship with the class, or with any individual within that class. It is through such a display of confidence that the barriers of erroneously perceived authoritarianism begin to dissolve.

Using humour to alter status, in a similar manner to the way in which one may choose to be diminutive in terms of body language, affects the teacher's perceived and their real status. A teacher who is able to laugh at themselves is no longer a despot to be undermined, nor are they an under-confident intern desperately and defensively combing over their flaws in the vain hope the class will not discover them.

In laughing at yourself first, you are opening yourself up, becoming human. You are identifying the sweet spot and quietly informing the class that (there it is), here is my most vulnerable point; I am sufficiently comfortable and at ease in this situation to reveal it to you. Do your worst.

(By the way what's yours? Let's be flawed together. Let's share important stuff with each other. Let's be empathetic and let's have a laugh!)

Laughter may temporarily dissolve whatever problematic baggage your students have brought into the lesson with them. It helps us to forget, and each laugh at a difficult situation chips away at its power to hurt or to damage. A lesson that starts with laughter, early on, will rid any individual member of your class of whatever anticipated concerns they may have.

This is one of the reasons that the routine of greeting your class at the door is such a vital part of your teaching armoury. Your ready smile at the door at the beginning of each lesson and, particularly their expectation of it as standard, creates engagement and scaffolds their day (provided everyone does it). In doing it, you are also able to check the temperature of the kids as they enter. If there has been anything fractious that has occurred outside of the classroom environment, which threatens to spill over into it, you will be more likely to sense it if you are at the door smiling, than if you are crouched over your desk putting the last twists to a comprehension worksheet.

Here we are reminded of Haim Ginott's statement: 'I've come to the frightening conclusion that I am the decisive element in the classroom. It's my daily mood that makes the weather.'[4] Stand at the door, smiling, every lesson, and you create an expectation that the weather in your class is always sunny.

---

[4] Ginott, 1975.

Laughter for different purposes

Just as we laugh at different things, so laughter can be used for different purposes. It can be used both environmentally and individually, at initial stages and later on in the relationship with a particular class or individual student. The important thing is its effect: what it can be made to do with the right tweaks and understanding.

It transforms a work environment into a play environment

A friend of ours who works in an environment that you would ordinarily expect to be rather more starchy than a school – he works in a starch factory – once came up with the line that initially feels like one of Ricky Gervais's cast-offs, 'Work's got to be fun; otherwise it's just that … work!'

If we refer back to the ideal *flow* state covered in the Introduction, laughter is the great way of stopping us (humans) from being aware that we are, in fact, in an unconducive building doing something we have to do because other people have said that we have to do it. The ecstatic blast of laughter transforms the bleakest of environments into a playground and is the most elegant and powerful riposte to the idea that the Scottish intellectual, Pat Kane, in his masterful and exhaustive volume on play, *The Play Ethic*, ably satirizes as being that, 'Work, no matter how alienating or ill-suited to temperament, is noble in and of itself.'[5]

The benefits of playfulness in the classroom and, indeed, in any environment are well attested.

Play makes you live longer. Play helps women select a trustworthy mate (men who are playful, or who can play with children, are less likely to be rapists or murderers). Play for adults improves their memories; it can make them happier, more elated … the opposite of play isn't work. It's depression.[6]

And the scientific evidence also points to its efficacy:

The science is clear on this: play is good for all young, warm-blooded organisms. The consensus from biologists and psychologists, derived

---

[5] Kane, 2005, p. 13.
[6] Kane, 2005, p. 44.

from over a century of observing animal and human play, is that play is a necessity, not a luxury, for advanced mammals. It is the way we test out our strategies for survival and reproduction at an early and crucial stage, in an environment relatively free from risk. By helping to make us capable organisms, play therefore ensures the progress of ourselves, our society and our species.[7]

However, to continue with a brief examination of how a 'ludic' classroom is one in which behavioural issues are less likely to occur, we must also acknowledge that in hierarchical organizations ruled by men or women with clipboards a playful attitude can be distrusted. As Kane suggests organizations can regard play as, 'This radioactive, fissile element: an energy source, sure, but one which – if it isn't properly contained and harnessed – could irradiate the entire place and melt down all existing boundaries.'[8] It is true that play must be within boundaries, but do not let the fact that your 'play' with your students has to operate within a professional structure affect your level of playfulness, or how hard and long you are prepared to laugh.

It can be used to open relationships

A little one-liner when you are meeting a new class can work wonders. The most successful of these that Phil has ever used is to introduce himself as 'someone who is meant to be one of the best teachers in the country, but (as you'll soon find out), clearly isn't!' John recalls inviting a class in ahead of him and saying, 'Age before beauty.' And waiting just about the amount of time it has taken you to read this sentence before the students realized what he said was entirely wrong and smirking accordingly. The line 'Do you speak English?' to someone who clearly does is quite a decent opening gambit, and has been known to cause the most closed of children to open up instantaneously.

---

[7] Kane, 2005, p. 41.
[8] Kane, 2005, p. 12.

Versions of humour – surrealism in the classroom

The behaviour management expert, Sue Cowley, whose book *Getting the Buggers to Behave* is on many university reading lists, receives the odd brickbat, not only for the title of her book, but also for the light-hearted suggestion it makes that a sound piece of behavioural management advice is to take in a tin of dog food and to pretend to eat dog food from it. We will leave Sue to clarify:

> The can had actually been cleaned out and refilled with a mix of Mars Bars and jelly, which when mashed together look surprisingly convincing. The lesson itself was about packaging, and in particular looking at a few important points: (1) How do we ensure that packaging is tamper proof? (2) Should you always believe what you read on a label? and (3) How are you affected by the marketing of a product? Of course the initial response from the children was, 'Urrggghhh, what are you doing, Sir!!???' But eventually they did quiet [sic] down because they were so curious to see what was actually going on. And after that lesson – oh the buzz that was created in the corridors of the school. Yes, it's the 'edge of madness' style of teaching, but what a way to get yourself a reputation for doing interesting lessons![9]

Her suggestion has been felt by many to be too wildly left-field to be of any serious use. However, there is a kernel of an idea here: the surrealist gesture in a classroom can be a brilliant way of twisting the status quo and manipulating the class's mass opinion of the teacher.[10]

Mild displays of surrealist humour are certainly of use in the classroom. The best, most gentle and quietest of these are charming word plays, or deliberate misunderstandings and mispronunciations, exploiting language's ambiguities. A former colleague used to delight in calling the register out in spoonerisms: Barlie Clake for Charlie Blake, Gerry Tibson for Terry Gibson, until such time as he had a student in his class called Kelly Smunt,

---

[9] www.suecowley.co.uk/lessons-i-love.html
[10] Though there is a very good chance that, if you eat dog food in a lesson, you will be sacked for going against the school's healthy eating policy; as well as being a little too mental for teaching.

when all laughing had to stop altogether. As Barry Blake says in *Playing with Words*:

> Exploiting the humorous possibilities of language obviously provides entertainment, but people also use verbal humour for other ends: to establish harmony or rapport, to ingratiate themselves, to lighten the mood when contentious issues are raised, and to soften the force of criticism.[11]

A particularly gentle version of humour which works in the classroom is the use of non sequiters. This is a kind of anti joke, containing some kind of causal fallacy and requiring a period of take-up time for the person hearing it, for example:

'Friends are like potatoes, if you eat them, they die.'

'Why did the chicken cross the road? Because he felt like it. Why does everything the chicken does have to be examined?'

Its use marks the teacher out as being prone to daftness, which, in case you were wondering, is a good thing.

For some teachers the imperative of daftness is quite easy to obey: for others, however, it comes less easily. Both of us find that being idiotic comes quite naturally and have, after a settling-in period, found it relatively easy to launch into absurd and deliberately badly sung improvised songs about a particular aspect of a student's behaviour. But, as a tactic, being completely idiotic is not a first-lesson gambit: it has to wait till there is a gathering body of opinion in the classroom that sir or miss is probably all right, and should be used to cement this as an idea and to make the atmosphere in the room light-hearted, to defuse any tensions you may recognize are bubbling under the surface. You can't start a fight when you're laughing.

Using humour as a punishment

It may quite reasonably be argued that many teachers' senses of humour are, themselves, a punishment designed especially for their students. We have found that we have got less funny as we have got older, and that this has even become the subject of mocking banter from students: 'Man, I musta been

---

[11] Blake, 2007, p. x.

at this school a long time, sir: I remember you from when you was funny!'
And there is certainly a sense that as your face fades into invisibility to the
opposite sex, you are perceived as being less funny.

If you are going to take punitive action it can be a good idea to make
the punishment itself humorous. The 'punishment as futile task' technique
goes back to the days when qualifications were actually worth the paper they
were written on. It is the trick of a 1970s Welsh metalwork teacher who set
students punishments of writing essays on the sex life of a teapot/bicycle
seat/ping pong ball, and would be regarded by many as unprofessional.
Whatever the politics of it, as a technique it works quite well. Students see
little real offence in it, and it will mark you out, not only as someone who
will certainly follow through with a threatened punishment, but also as
someone who will do it in a light-hearted way.

Exploiting humour that relies on a delay in take-up

A widower buys a parrot. When he gets it home he puts it on a perch and sits
back in his velvet armchair to admire its plumage. Wondering if the parrot
can talk he starts playing with clichés: 'Who's a pretty boy then?' he asks.

The parrot looks at him and then squawks a word so obscene that no lady
ever likes to hear it used. The lonely widower looks aghast, as he fears that
the widow who lives next door will hear the parrot. The parrot continues
swearing at the top of its voice every puce curse it is able to muster.

In panic, the widower takes the parrot into the garden, and into the shed,
and locks the door. Still the parrot, this time louder still, continues to run
through a volley of every possible combination of foul language: it squawks
curse upon curse. Exasperated, and desperate that the next-door widow's ears
are not besmirched by such a foul display of sexual swear words, he bundles
the parrot up and puts it into the fridge, just to give himself a brief respite.

Immediately, the swearing stops.

Ten minutes of silence later the lonely widower opens the fridge door to
see a penitent parrot, his wings raised in supplication. 'Look,' says the parrot
clearly shaken, 'I'm sorry. I'm aware that my language was completely
beyond the pale. I promise that I will never swear again. Just put me on the
perch and I'll sing like a canary.'

Surprised, the lonely widower puts the parrot back on the perch. 'By the way,' asks the parrot, 'what did the chicken do?'

It is the two or three seconds that it takes for this joke to work that puts it among one of our favourite jokes. And this particular technique, of making students think ('Hold on, that's ... ah!'), can be used in the early stages of an interaction with any class to shift the tectonic plates of status-based relationships. It is by deliberately saying things that causes students to think, 'Hold on ...' that you can rebalance the power dynamic and can let them know that they are dealing with someone with a sense of humour.

Good and bad laughter

But there is good laughter and there is bad laughter. As Australian academic Barry Blake so rightly points out, 'There is (thus) a negative side to humour. It can be used to deride, to mock, to belittle, to stereotype.'[12] As such, there are certain *don'ts* as regarding your use of humour that you should obey as cardinal rules.

If we go back to Haim Ginott's famous aphorism, he extends it into musing that, 'As a teacher, I possess a tremendous power to make a child's life miserable or joyous. I can be a tool of torture or an instrument of inspiration. I can humiliate or humour, hurt or heal. In all situations, it is my response that decides whether a crisis will be escalated or de-escalated and a child humanized or de-humanized.'[13]

It is the closeness of 'humiliate or humour, hurt or heal' that is of interest in terms of your use of humour in a classroom. The words are presented, deliberately we think, as juxtaposed, related opposites: it is your decision whether to use laughter for fair or for foul means, whether to use it to humour and heal, or to humiliate and hurt.

Even Jimmy Carr, a comedian who has achieved fame for punchlines about the Variety Club's Sunshine vans for children with Down's Syndrome, and who is responsible for the following line: 'Say what you like about the servicemen amputees from Iraq and Afghanistan but we're going to have a f***ing good

---

[12] Blake, 2007, p. xi.
[13] Ginott, 1975.

Paralympics team,'[14] acknowledges laughter's ability to hurt. He says, 'There are some jokes which are downright evil, whether we like it or not. A joke can be little more than an insult, a socially sanctioned cruelty. Jokes can make people feel threatened and they can make people very angry.'[15]

One of your chief values as a teacher must be, first, to do no harm. Your use of humour must come with an awareness of the fact that if used improperly it can do immense damage. As a practitioner you will do well to be aware of two cardinal rules:

1   Do laugh at the ball or at yourself. Do not laugh at the kids. You may laugh with them if they are laughing at themselves, but you must not be the instigator of that laughter and certainly you should not be at the centre of everyone else laughing at one person.

2   Don't employ sarcasm. Though it is tempting, when some idiot intones that it is the lowest form of wit, to reply that just because something is easy it doesn't mean it isn't worth doing, in the classroom it really is a scoundrel's trick to take cheap sarcastic pot-shots at the developing emotional landscape of a child for having bravely embraced the failure in the manner you've been asking for for the last six months. Being a child at the receiving end of an adult's sarcasm is a dark and powerless place to live, and you should not even give a child the briefest of weekend breaks there. And if you find yourself being sarcastic about the work a child has done, if they have put their soul into it, then DO beat yourself up about it ... and then forgive yourself ... and don't do it again.

Test yourself

Can you use humour to create relationships?				
I can be self-deprecating.				

---

[14] http://current.com/shows/current-tonight/91291179_was-jimmy-carrs-amputee-joke-offensive-or-armless.htm
[15] Carr and Greeves, 2007, p. 7.

My classroom is a playful arena.				
I use humour to fostor relationships.				
I am prepared to use humour when issuing sanctions.				
I am aware of the difference between 'good' and 'bad' humour.				

Conclusion

We started this book with a description of how the experience, and the symbiosis, of teaching and learning can be rapturous; and it can ...

But in certain circumstances, in certain environments, it can also verge on the horrendous.

If you are working in a school in which the management team are in no way on top of behaviour; if the kids' education has, historically, been so stunted that, it seems, the whole culture of the school is anti-achievement, and if it is the children who rule the roost, you will struggle. If you are working in a school in which the only thing that remotely counts with the kids is the number of years you have been there, and 'teacher abuse' is a routine part of daily school life, it can be like being plunged into an inferno on a daily basis and you may find yourself coming home having been so used to conducting yourself in an environment of naked aggression that you become very difficult indeed to live with.

If you are working in that kind of school, the things you have learnt through the process of reading this book will not instantaneously solve things, they will not make the children you teach sit up and perform Pavlovian tricks, and they will not make your lessons immediately easier. Life – particularly the managing behaviour in a challenging school part of it – isn't that easy. Hell, no.

When dealing with the worst behaviour, you must remember to give yourself time. It takes time to work through some behaviour issues, and it is the passage of time that is your best friend. Give yourself an allotted period of time and then look at it again. Say to yourself, for example: 'This is how I feel about things now. I will feel differently after I've completed the first half term.' Don't leave when it gets rough; it will get better. When John started working at the behavioural unit he gave himself a time frame of a year and a half before he would look at how he felt things were going: 18 months to get the students to a position where they were starting to manage their own behaviour. You will not sort out complex, deeply held institutional issues by yourself in a month. Don't be quite so naïve.

The two teachers who have written this book have over 35 combined years of experience of working in challenging environments, and what we have written here is the best that we have. That is not to say that we still don't have days where nothing seems to work, or that these techniques work all of the time in every given situation. That said, they will (if you apply them consistently) make you significantly better at managing behaviour in a challenging school than you were before you read this book. At this point it's worth going back to the questionnaire you completed at the end of the introduction and compare it to the knowledge you are now in possession of: you'll see that you've acquired quite a substantial body of knowledge through reading this book. Now you have to put it into practice. As we have said, it won't all change immediately. But apply the lessons consistently, keep examining your own behaviour, give yourself time, and you'll get there.

Good luck, and if it all gets too much, have a read of the following words. In moments of extreme stress, they might just give you enough help or inspiration to get up and into school the next morning.

1. People are illogical, unreasonable, and self-centered. Love them anyway.
2. If you do good, people will accuse you of selfish ulterior motives. Do good anyway.
3. If you are successful, you will win false friends and true enemies. Succeed anyway.
4. The good you do today will be forgotten tomorrow. Do good anyway.
5. Honesty and frankness make you vulnerable. Be honest and frank anyway.
6. The biggest men and women with the biggest ideas can be shot down by the smallest men and women with the smallest minds. Think big anyway.
7. People favor underdogs but follow only top dogs. Fight for a few underdogs anyway.
8. What you spend years building may be destroyed overnight. Build anyway.
9. People really need help but may attack you if you do help them. Help people anyway.
10. Give the world the best you have and you'll get kicked in the teeth. Give the world the best you have anyway.[1]

---

[1] 'The Paradoxical Commandments', Keith, Dr. Kent M., 1968.

References and further reading

Auchincloss, Eve (1981). Review of *Hands* by John Napier. New York: Pantheon Books.

Blake, Barry (2007). *Playing with Words – Humour in the English Language*. London: Equinox.

Bukowski, Charles (1966). 'The Genius of the Crowd'.

Carr, Jimmy and Greeves, Lucy (2007). *The Naked Jape: Uncovering the Hidden World of Jokes*. Penguin.

Chesterton, G. K. (1908). *Orthodoxy*. New York: Dodd, Mead & Co.

Cowley, S. (2010). *Getting the Buggers to Behave* (4th edn). Continuum: London.

Dalai Lama and Stril-Rever, Sofia (2010). *My Spiritual Journey*. New York: HarperOne.

DeSteno, David, Dasgupta, Nilanjana, Bartlett, Monica Y. and Cajdric, Aida (2004). 'Prejudice from Thin Air: The Effect of Emotion on Automatic Intergroup Attitudes', *Psychological Science* 15 (5): 319–24.

Eastman, Max (1939). *Enjoyment of Laughter*. New York: Halcyon House.

Echo and the Bunnymen (1981). 'Show of Strength', Mute Records.

Ekman, Paul (2004). *Emotions Revealed: Understanding Faces and Feelings*. London: Phoenix.

Ginott, Haim G. (1975). *Teacher and Child: A Book for Parents and Teachers*. New York: Macmillan.

Goleman, Daniel (1995). *Emotional Intelligence – Why It Can Matter More Than IQ*. New York: Bantam Books.

Harlow, Harry (1958). 'The Nature of Love', *American Psychologist* 13: 673–85.

Heslin, R. (1974). 'Steps Towards a Taxonomy of Touching'. Paper presented to the annual meeting of the Midwestern Psychological Association Chicago, Ilinois.

Jones, S. E. and Yarborough, A. E. (1985). 'A Naturalistic Study of the Meanings of Touch', *Communication Monographs*, 52: 19–56.

Kane, Pat (2005). *The Play Ethic*. Pan MacMillan.

Keeling, Dave and Hodgson, David (2011). *Invisible Teaching*. Wales, UK: Crown House.

Kent, Dr. Keith, (1968). The Paradoxical Commandments, *The Silent Revolution: Dynamic Leadership in the Student Council* Cambridge, Massachusetts: Harvard Student Agencies. www.paradoxicalcommandments.com

Mehrabian, Albert (1971). *Silent Messages* (1st edn). Belmont, CA: Wadsworth.

Rosenthal, Robert and Jacobson, Leonore (1992). *Pygmalion in the Classroom: Teacher Expectation and Pupil's Intellectual Development*. Wales, UK: Crown House.

School of Education, University of Bristol (1997). The Bristol Guide: Teachers' Legal Liabilities and Responsibilities DfEE Circular 10/97.

Sharot, Tali (2012). *The Optimism Bias – Why We're Wired to Look on the Bright Side*. London: Constable & Robinson.

Walton, D. (1989). *Are You Communicating? You Can't Manage without It*. New York: McGraw-Hill.

Wilson, Gary (2006). *Breaking Through Barriers to Boys' Achievement: Developing a Caring Masculinity*. London: Continuum.

— (2008). *Help Your Boys Succeed: The Essential Guide for Parents*. London: Continuum.

Index